SpringerBriefs in Economic

More information about this series at http://www.springer.com/series/8876

Bruno S. Frey

Economics of Happiness

Springer

Bruno S. Frey
University of Basel
Basel, Switzerland

and

CREMA, Center for Research in Economics,
Management and the Arts
Zurich, Switzerland

ISSN 2191-5504 ISSN 2191-5512 (electronic)
SpringerBriefs in Economics
ISBN 978-3-319-75806-0 ISBN 978-3-319-75807-7 (eBook)
https://doi.org/10.1007/978-3-319-75807-7

Library of Congress Control Number: 2018932523

Printed on acid-free paper

This Springer imprint is published by the registered company Springer International Publishing AG part of Springer Nature
The registered company address is: Gewerbestrasse 11, 6330 Cham, Switzerland

Acknowledgements

I am grateful for helpful discussions with Alois Stutzer and Margit Osterloh as well as with many other colleagues too numerous to mention individually. Thanks to Evelyn Holderegger and Simon Milligan for effective support in preparing and improving the manuscript.

Contents

1 Happiness as a Goal of Human Beings 1
Concepts of Happiness 1
Happiness and Material Welfare 2
Literature 4

2 Happiness Can Be Measured 5
Various Kinds of Happiness 5
Measurement Methods 6
Surveys of Subjective Life Satisfaction 7
U-Index 9
Experience Sampling Method 9
Day Reconstruction Method 9
Brain Activity 10
Literature 11

3 What Makes People Happy? 13
Determinants of Happiness 13
Genetic Endowment 14
Economic Factors 14
Income 14
Work 15
Distribution of Income 16
Economic Development 16
Socio-Demographic Influences 17
Age 17
Family Status 17
Children 17
Social Relationships 18
Health 18

Education . . . 18
Culture and Religion . . . 18
Political Conditions . . . 19
Democracy and Well-Being . . . 19
Federalism . . . 20
Literature . . . 20

4 **Consequences of Happiness** . . . 21
The Importance of Several Joint Influences . . . 21
The Effects of Happiness . . . 22
Causality . . . 23
Literature . . . 23

5 **Psychological Influences on Happiness** . . . 25
Happiness Is Partly Self-constructed . . . 25
Adaptation . . . 25
Comparison with Other People and Situations . . . 26
Cognitive Biases . . . 26
Restricted Prognostic Abilities . . . 27
Literature . . . 27

6 **Happiness Maximization by the Government** . . . 29
Should Politicians Maximize Happiness? . . . 29
Biased Answers to Happiness Surveys . . . 30
Manipulated Happiness Index . . . 30
Literature . . . 31

7 **What Happiness Policy Is Appropriate?** . . . 33
Enabling Happiness . . . 33
Happiness as Ultimate Goal? . . . 33
Institutions Leading to Happiness . . . 34
Happiness in the Current Politico-Economic Process . . . 36
Job Market and Economic Growth . . . 36
Income Inequality . . . 37
Independence and Self-employment . . . 38
Voluntary Work and Donations . . . 38
Family and Social Relationships . . . 38
Education . . . 39
Liveable Cities . . . 39
Literature . . . 39

8 **What About a Happiness Pill?** . . . 41
Happiness Pills Exist . . . 41
A Thought Experiment . . . 41
Positive Effects . . . 42

Negative Effects . . . 43
Substitutes and Complements . . . 43
Procedural Benefits . . . 44
The Paradox of Happiness . . . 44
Selfish Governments . . . 44
What Can Be Said? . . . 45
Literature . . . 46

9 Happiness and Consumption . . . 47
Welfare Judgments . . . 47
Limited Self-control and Individual Well-Being . . . 47
Misprediction of Utility . . . 48
Literature . . . 49

10 Happiness and Television Viewing . . . 51
An Important Consumption Activity . . . 51
Effects of Television Watching on Happiness . . . 52
Effects Differ Between Groups . . . 53
Literature . . . 54

11 Happiness and Management . . . 55
Effects of Happiness on Business Activities . . . 55
Instrumental Use of Happiness . . . 56
Various Forms of Happiness . . . 56
Offering Possibilities for Happiness . . . 57
Literature . . . 58

12 Happiness and Religion . . . 59
Models of Religious Activity . . . 59
Types of Religiosity . . . 60
Internal Religiosity: Faith . . . 60
External Religiosity: Attending Church Service . . . 60
Denomination . . . 61
Effect Size . . . 61
Literature . . . 62

13 Happiness and War . . . 63
Fundamentals . . . 63
The Well-Being Lost by the Dead . . . 65
Disregarding the Well-Being of the Dead by Definition . . . 66
The Case of Terrorism . . . 67
Military Conflict May Raise Happiness . . . 67
Psychological Costs of Military Combat . . . 69
Concluding Remarks . . . 69
Literature . . . 70

14 Happiness in the Digital World 71
Internet Use 71
Literature 72

15 Beyond Material Aspects 73
Expected and Unexpected Insights 73
Literature 75

Chapter 1
Happiness as a Goal of Human Beings

Abstract There are many concepts and ideas regarding what happiness may mean, but it certainly is a major goal of human beings. In the past, the concept of Gross National Product (GNP) was an important social innovation for capturing economic activity. A higher material living standard enabled people to lead better and healthier lives. Many people have a romantic view of the quality of life in previous centuries. However, people living in those times had no access to material things nowadays taken for granted. Similarly, goods and services that are generally available in the developed world may be inaccessible for many in the developing world. Today, it is no longer assumed that higher material wealth automatically leads to higher life satisfaction. There are many other factors that determine happiness beyond purely material aspects. It is important to deal with the fundamental questions of how much material consumption contributes to our happiness and which factors above and beyond material aspects determine human well-being.

Concepts of Happiness

When you ask people what they want to be, they rarely say that they want to be rich or prominent. Instead, most of them declare that they want to be happy. In all periods in history, and in all countries, a large majority of people express their desire to lead a happy life. They certainly acknowledge that there are other worthy goals, such as human development, justice, friendship, and solidarity. Even when these other goals are considered to be important, happiness dominates them, or they are taken to be a particular subcategory of happiness.

While happiness is the major goal of most people, what "happiness" means remains open. Its meaning certainly depends on the period in history and on the culture considered. Philosophers of ancient Greece such as Aristotle emphasized that a happy person acts in a moral way; individual happiness was not primordial. For medieval scholars such as Saint Thomas Aquinas, the relationship to god was essential. Ethical, ideological, and political views in China and East Asia put the

B. S. Frey, *Economics of Happiness*, SpringerBriefs in Economics,
https://doi.org/10.1007/978-3-319-75807-7_1

relationship between people in the centre and so focus on the quality of life within a society.

Today's understanding of happiness is mainly individualistic. People's well-being entails an evaluation of good and bad aspects of life. It is not reduced to psychological hedonism but refers to the satisfaction people gain when they reach, for instance, desired goals. Psychological Self-Determination Theory proposes that three psychological requirements must be satisfied to be happy: autonomy, competence, and personal relationships. All three are closely connected with intrinsic, rather than extrinsic, motivation.

Happiness and Material Welfare

For a long time, it was taken as self-evident that higher material wealth automatically leads to more life satisfaction. During the Second World War, the concept of national income or national product was developed. This was a major social innovation that for the first time enabled overall economic activity to be measured. Gross National Product (GNP) includes the production of consumption and investment, goods and services produced for markets, and expenditures on government activity. GNP captures the material activities undertaken in a society quite well. Increasing welfare was identified by an increase in GNP mainly because it was considered impossible to measure the aggregate utility of human beings. In particular, the problem of comparing the utility of different people was taken to be too difficult to overcome. Even today, the public and the media often take per capita GNP as a good approximation to welfare. When it rises over time, it supposedly indicates that population enjoys a higher utility standard. When countries are compared, those with a higher per capita GNP are considered to be better off.

The identification of per capita GNP with life satisfaction has been common in much of economic science and the public and has been widely accepted. A higher material living standard certainly enables people to lead better and healthier lives. This can be disputed. Nonetheless, many people have a romantic view of the quality of life in previous centuries. Would it not be nice to live in the time of Aristotle in Athens, in Caesar's Rome, in the Europe of Charles the Great, in the blooming Weimar of Goethe and Schiller, in England during the reign of Elisabeth I, or in Washington during the foundation of the United States? Such a view is, however, mistaken if we focus on the conditions of life of people during these periods.

People living in those times had no access to material things that today are taken for granted. For instance, our ancestors did not have any of the following amenities:

- Electricity and thus light, telephone, radio, TV, refrigerators, X-rays, as well as the revolutionary changes brought about by the digital world through computers and the Internet;
- Easy and comfortable opportunities to travel by bikes, cars, trains and airplanes;

- Synthetic materials such as plastic, nylon, vinyl, and the many thousands of products using these such as CDs and artificial joints.

All these products, and a great many others, were not available to anyone—at any price. Even only 150 years ago, not even the richest and most powerful individuals could buy antibiotic medicine to fight and overcome a bacterial illness, and lifesaving penicillin was not yet available. Generally, medical support was miserable. The same applies to dentistry. When a tooth was ailing, it was simply, and painfully, extracted. This happened to the "Roi Soleil" of France, Louis XIV. During a brutal medical intervention, a large part of his jawbone was also extracted. For the rest of his life, this mighty king could no longer chew food. The sanitary conditions in the fantastic palace of Versailles, as well as at Hampton Court, or elsewhere, can only be described as abominable.

From the material point of view, the world is today in a far better condition than it was even a century ago. Nowadays, a family with middle or even low income has a better chance to lead a comfortable life than even kings and emperors had in earlier times. This material improvement is reflected in a dramatic increase in life expectancy. Not long ago, the average life expectancy was about 30 years. Of course, some people became "old", but this meant reaching an age of 50 or 60. Not least because people lost their teeth early, older age was easily visible. A large proportion of the population died as babies or young children. Today, global average life expectancy at birth is over 65 years, in rich countries around 80 years.

In recent decades, it has increasingly been doubted whether material welfare really makes us content. It is argued that "true" happiness comes from inside a person and therefore does not depend on material conditions. Such statements often come from people who are well off—at least in a historical perspective. The economic basis of our well-being is often taken as given; it just exists. Today, there is a wide consensus that to concentrate only on material welfare is mistaken. The consumption of material goods and services alone cannot lead to happiness.

For these reasons, it is important to deal with the fundamental questions of how much material consumption contributes to our happiness and which factors above and beyond material consumption determine human well-being.

Discussions about happiness in academia and the public have gained widespread attention. The media are full of articles about who is how happy, and above all, how to become happy. Research has addressed these issues intensively. Interdisciplinary happiness research is undertaken by social psychologists, economists, political scientists, sociologists, and neuroscientists. It is strongly empirically oriented. In this respect, it differs fundamentally from philosophy, a discipline that has always dealt with happiness analytically as a normative phenomenon.

Literature

Surveys of happiness research are available in the following books.

The economic perspective is given in:

Clark, Andrew E., Sarah Flèche, Richard Layard, Nattavudh Powdthavee, and George Ward. 2017. *The Origins of Happiness. The Science of Well-Being over the Life Course*. Princeton: Princeton University Press.

Frey, Bruno S., and Alois Stutzer. 2002a. *Happiness and Economics*. Princeton: Princeton University Press.

Frey, Bruno S. 2008. *Happiness—A Revolution in Economics*. Cambridge, Mass.: MIT Press.

Layard, Richard. 2005. *Happiness: Lessons from a New Science*. London: Penguin.

The psychological perspective is presented in:

Diener, Ed and Robert Biswas-Diener. 2008. *Happiness: Unlocking the Mysteries of Psychological Wealth*. New York: Wiley.

Gilbert, Daniel. 2005. *Stumbling on Happiness*. New York: Knopf.

Kahneman, Daniel, Ed Diener, and Norbert Schwarz (eds.). 1999. *Well-Being: The Foundations of Hedonic Psychology*. New York: Russell Sage Foundation.

Survey articles in academic journals and handbooks include:

Dolan, Paul, Tessa Peasgood, and Mathew White. 2008. Do We Really Know What Makes Us Happy? A Review of the Economic Literature on the Factors Associated with Subjective Well-being. *Journal of Economic Psychology* 29 (1): 94–122.

Frey, Bruno S., and Alois Stutzer. 2002b. What Can Economists Learn from Happiness Research? *Journal of Economic Literature* 40 (2): 402–435.

Various articles are collected in:

Bruni, Luigino, and Pier Luigi Porta (eds.). 2005. *Economics and Happiness. Framing the Analysis*. Oxford: Oxford University Press.

David, Susan A., Ilona Boniwell, and Amanda Conley Ayers (eds.). 2017. *The Oxford Handbook of Happiness*. Oxford: Oxford University Press.

Easterlin, Richard (ed.). 2002. *Happiness in Economics*. Cheltenham UK: Edward Elgar.

Frey, Bruno S., and Alois Stutzer (eds.). 2013. *Recent Developments in the Economics of Happiness*. Cheltenham UK: Edward Elgar.

Chapter 2
Happiness Can Be Measured

Abstract Most empirical research uses subjective and self-reported life satisfaction to capture happiness. The answers correspond well to everyday observations about what well-being means. Subjective life satisfaction data are presented here for several countries. People living in the Nordic countries, above all Denmark and Switzerland, are the happiest. The nations in which the average life satisfaction of its inhabitants is lowest are, with the exception of Syria, all situated in Africa. Happiness can also be measured by other methods such as the *U-index*, which captures the periods of a day in which individuals surveyed felt that they were in an "unpleasant state"; *experience sampling*, which is an electronic diary capturing immediate, affective experiences; *day reconstruction*, which retrospectively reconstructs subjective feelings through the various phases of a day; and *brain imaging*, which employs functional magnetic resonance imaging (fMRI) to capture the brain activity of human beings with respect to positive and negative affect.

Various Kinds of Happiness

It is useful to distinguish between several aspects of happiness.

Two extreme forms of happiness may be distinguished:

- *Momentary feelings* of pleasure, in psychology called "positive affect", and of distress, called "negative affect";
- Beatitude, or eternal bliss, in Greek called "*eudaimonia*". It is a by-product of a good and moral life. This is the state of mind which one would consider shortly before dying if one were asked how one's life had been, or whether it had been worthwhile to have lived. Eudaimonia is associated with six components of positive human functioning: autonomy, emphasizing independent, self-regulating and self-determined aspects of life; environmental mastery, characterized by a fit between one's outer and inner worlds; personal growth, meaning self-realization and achieving one's personal potential; positive relations with others, based on the human ability to love others; purpose of life and meaning, involving a sense of directness

B. S. Frey, *Economics of Happiness*, SpringerBriefs in Economics,
https://doi.org/10.1007/978-3-319-75807-7_2

and intentionality to life; and self-acceptance of present and past life, enabling people to mature and remain in good mental health.

Empirical research in happiness focuses on an intermediate form of happiness, *subjective life satisfaction*. It reflects the answers given to the question: "Taken overall, how satisfied are you with the life you lead?" Individuals answering this question abstract from purely short-run feelings because they are asked to consider their situation "overall", and with respect to "the life you lead", neither do they ponder on their whole life in retrospect.

Another distinction emphasizes the temporal dimension of subjective well-being:

- *Experienced happiness* as a short-run psychological state of mind;
- *Predicted* or *expected* happiness; and
- *Remembered happiness* referring to the past.

Psychologists have shown us that human beings deal quite differently with these dimensions of happiness. Thus, for example, expected happiness may deviate strongly from the happiness that is actually experienced. People may also remember their past happiness quite differently from what they actually felt when it occurred.

Despite its many dimensions, happiness can be measured quantitatively in a meaningful way. Social psychology has extensively discussed which approaches are useful. Measured subjective well-being (this is the scientific term for "happiness") is characterized by three aspects:

- The measures are not in any way meant to be objective. Rather, happiness is taken to be a subjective state of mind;
- Both positive and negative influences on happiness are considered; and
- Happiness is taken as a whole; it is not confined to any special area of life, such as satisfaction with one's job, with leisure, or with the financial situation.

The well-being values measured correspond well with everyday ideas about how happy people are. Individuals who consider themselves happier than average are also taken to be happier than average by other people. Their partners, family, and friends rank them as particularly happy. Individuals that indicate that they are satisfied with their lives smile more often (in a way that cannot be faked); are more open; establish more social contacts; are in better health; and need less psychic support. They are also less prone to committing suicide.

Measurement Methods

Modern happiness research employs a subjective concept of happiness; every person must establish himself or herself what happiness means to him or her. Such an approach can measure happiness in various ways. The measurement methods capture the two basic components of happiness: affect and cognition. Affect relates to moods and feelings, and these can be positive or negative. The cognitive aspect refers to the rational and intellectual way in which human beings evaluate their subjective well-being.

Surveys of Subjective Life Satisfaction

Happiness is measured by extensive surveys of a representative group of people. Careful questions are used to collect the self-evaluated well-being of individuals. This involves a cognitive process in which the respondents undertake comparisons with others, consider experiences in the past, and evaluate expectations in the future.

The question capturing subjective life satisfaction is:

> Taken overall, how satisfied are you with the life you lead on a scale from 0 (totally dissatisfied) to 10 (totally satisfied)?

This question about subjective well-being entails considerations over an extended period of time, as it refers to "the life you lead", and to a general assessment, as it refers to "taken overall". As a result, the responses differ little when the same respondents are asked again in subsequent periods of time. If one were to ask people how "happy" they are, the answers might be strongly influenced by short run emotions and passing external influences. Thus, persons take themselves to be happier when the weather is fine than when it is bad. Consequently, the question asking respondents to indicate their life satisfaction is more reliable than one asking them to indicate their affective happiness.

The distribution of answers given by respondents about their subjective life satisfaction is quite surprising: Most people consider themselves to be happy.

The United Nations published a *World Happiness Report* for 2017. It presents the average subjective life satisfaction of the inhabitants of 155 countries on the scale from 0 (totally dissatisfied) to 10 (totally satisfied).

The happiest countries are:

Norway	7.54
Denmark	7.52
Iceland	7.50
Switzerland	7.49
Finland	7.47
Netherlands	7.40
Canada	7.32
New Zealand	7.32
Australia	7.28
Sweden	7.28

The countries with the happiest inhabitants are close together; there is only a minor difference between the very top (Norway with 7.54) and the tenth (Sweden with 7.28). All the five Nordic countries (Norway, Denmark, Iceland, Finland, Sweden) belong to the top ten happiest countries. Switzerland has always been ranked among the top, often even in first or second position together with Denmark. The former British colonies Canada, New Zealand, and Australia also rank among the top ten.

Countries ranked between 10 and 20 include:

Austria	7.01
United States	6.99
Ireland	6.98
Germany	6.95
United Kingdom	6.71

The difference from the top 10 is visible, but the average happiness level in the population is not much lower.

Among the least happy countries in Europe are the five Southern members of the European Union:

France	6.44
Spain	6.40
Italy	5.96
Greece	5.23
Portugal	5.20

These countries are located between position 31 for France and 89 for Portugal.

People living in countries formerly under Soviet rule report a rather lower level of subjective well-being:

Czech Republic	6.61
Poland	5.97
Russia	5.96
Romania	5.83
Belarus	5.57
Hungary	5.32
Bulgaria	4.71
Georgia	4.29

The Czech Republic stands out (position 23) as relatively satisfied while the inhabitants of Bulgaria and Georgia are quite dissatisfied with the life they lead (ranks 105 and 125). The Poles and Russians are reasonably happy (ranks 46 and 49, respectively) while the Hungarians are clearly less so (rank 75).

The nations in which the average life satisfaction of its inhabitants is lowest according to the World Happiness Report 2017 are the following developing countries, all situated in Africa with the exception of Syria:

Togo	3.50
Rwanda	3.47
Syria	3.46
Tanzania	3.35
Burundi	2.91
Central African Rep.	2.69

These countries occupy positions 150–155. The only country in which the population is equally dissatisfied with its life as in the five African countries mentioned is war-torn Syria, with a happiness index of 3.46 and rank 152.

These tables refute the idea that people living in economically less developed countries are happier because they are less subject to the stress of life typical in richer countries. Indeed, a large proportion of the people living in poor countries are deeply stressed by the effort of securing food and shelter for today and for coming weeks and months.

Nations involved in civil and international wars or that are subject to civil unrest experience lower material and psychological welfare. Examples are:

Ukraine	4.09
Afghanistan	3.79
Yemen	3.59
South Sudan	3.59

They rank between 132 (Ukraine) and 147 (South Sudan).

U-Index

This measure captures the periods of a day in which participants felt that they were in an "unpleasant state". This index has the advantage that it is able to capture a broader spectrum of happiness. In particular, it allows us to measure *or* to observe improvements in well-being more precisely because the scale less frequently reaches an upper limit than is the case for a scale from 0 to 10.

Experience Sampling Method

This measure identifies information about people's short-run subjective experiences. They are called on their mobile phones in a natural environment and at randomly distributed times and asked how happy they are at these moments. This electronic diary is a kind of "hedonimeter" that captures immediate, affective experiences. This method is more costly than representative surveys and has therefore been applied only rarely.

Day Reconstruction Method

Various phases over the course of a day are retrospectively specified. The respondents are asked how happy they felt during these phases. This method is based on time budgets that indicate how much time people spend on what activity. The retrospective reconstruction of subjective feelings through the various phases of a day makes it possible to measure happiness more precisely than with a representative survey using a single question. This approach to capturing happiness is rather new and has not yet been used extensively.

Brain Activity

Brain imaging employs functional magnetic resonance imaging (fMRI) to capture the brain activity of human beings, and this can be correlated with positive and negative affect. The application of this method is severely restricted for reasons of cost and cannot be used for a large sample of people in many different countries. To measure brain activity in this way can, however, be useful for specific questions relating to happiness.

The various measures capture different aspects of individual well-being and thus address different concepts of individual welfare. For a measure of reported subjective well-being to serve as a proxy for individual welfare, the standards underlying people's judgments should be those that the individual would like to pursue in realizing his or her ideal of the good life. The extent to which individual welfare is identified depends on whether the evaluation metric fits people's judgments about their lives.

Several other methods can be used to capture happiness. These approaches differ strongly from the method most often used—representative surveys of individuals asking for their life satisfaction. The latter approach has the great advantage that fundamental and well-considered answers can be collected about the subjective well-being of a large number of individuals. The respondents think about how they are satisfied with their lives as a whole and short-run influences are avoided. Several data sources exist that cover various time periods, such as the Gallup World Survey, the British Household Panel, and the German Socio-Economic Panel (G-SOEP). Each of them surveys many thousands of individuals. In the case of panel data, the same individuals are asked over many years. This makes it possible to capture the development of life satisfaction over the life course.

The method of surveying subjective life satisfaction is best suited to answering many important questions relating to human well-being. There is now widespread consensus among scholars that the data on life satisfaction are well able to capture information about people's well-being. This is indicated by the fact that they correlate well with qualities and behaviours generally associated with happiness. Reliability studies have found that reported subjective well-being is moderately stable yet sensitive to changing life circumstances. Happy people smile more often during social interactions, are rated as happy by friends and family members and by spouses, express positive emotions more frequently, are more optimistic, are more sociable and extravert, and sleep better. Happy people are also less likely to commit suicide.

For these reasons, the following discussion relies on this approach. In line with the literature, the terms well-being, happiness and life satisfaction will be used interchangeably.

Literature

A general discussion of measurement issues in connection with happiness is discussed in:

Weimann, Joachim, Andreas Knabe, and Ronnie Schöb. 2015. *Measuring Happiness. The Economics of Well-Being*. Cambridge MA: MIT Press.

An important contribution is provided by two Nobel Prize winners:

Deaton, Angus. 2008. Income, Health, and Well-Being around the World: Evidence from the Gallup World Poll. *Journal of Economic Perspectives* 22 (2): 53–72.
Kahneman, Daniel, and Alan B. Krueger. 2006. Developments in the Measurement of Subjective Well-Being. *Journal of Economic Perspectives* 20 (1): 3–24.

Fundamental issues of well-being are treated from a psychological perspective:

Ryff, Carol D. 2017. Eudaimonic Well-being, Inequality, and Health: Recent Findings and Future Directions. *International Review of Economics* 64 (2): 159–178.

Chapter 3
What Makes People Happy?

Abstract Happiness research determines, isolates, and measures the various determinants of human well-being. The data collected on the subjective life satisfaction of individuals are related to possible determinants of happiness by multiple regressions. The personality structure determined by one's genetic inheritance has a strong influence on happiness. Among economic factors, people with higher incomes unambiguously consider themselves to be more satisfied with their lives than do people with low income, and people losing their job are much more dissatisfied with their lives than are those holding a job. Prominent among the socio-demographic influences is a U-shaped relationship between age and life satisfaction; married people are happier than those living alone; and intensive and regular social contacts within the family and among friends and acquaintances contribute strongly to happiness. Physical and psychological health contribute strongly to well-being. Cultural differences matter, and religious persons are demonstrably happier than those who do not belong to a religious community. Happiness is positively influenced by democracy and political decentralization.

Determinants of Happiness

One of the most important tasks of happiness research consists in determining, isolating, and measuring the various determinants of human well-being. The data collected on the subjective life satisfaction of individuals are related to possible determinants of happiness by multiple regressions. Both simple and advanced nonlinear statistical techniques are used. What matters is that the influence of various factors is taken into account simultaneously. Many econometric estimates consider the joint effect of twenty, thirty, or even more variables. This procedure allows us to capture the *specific determinants* while keeping the influence of all other determinants constant. If, for instance, the impact of income on subjective well-being is analysed, age, family status, religion, and many other variables are kept constant. The results always refer to the average; it is therefore possible that the outcome deviates from this for an individual.

B. S. Frey, *Economics of Happiness*, SpringerBriefs in Economics,
https://doi.org/10.1007/978-3-319-75807-7_3

The following sections provide a short survey of the determinants of subjective life satisfaction in five different areas:

- Genetic endowment
- Economic factors
- Socio-demographic influences
- Culture and religion
- Political conditions.

Genetic Endowment

The personality structure determined by one's genetic inheritance has a strong influence on happiness. People differ by nature in respect to their well-being, and they have differing capacities to deal with their lives. Psychological studies suggest that the differences in happiness between persons that are attributable to variations in genetic inheritance amount to forty–sixty per cent of the total differences. Happiness is substantially determined by genetic factors. This statement can be illustrated by a concrete example. Of the people who break a leg, many who are genetically less favourably endowed are terribly unhappy about the incident. In contrast, those endowed with more optimism consider themselves lucky because they did not break both legs.

Nevertheless, there is a large residual going back to other influences on happiness.

Economic Factors

Income

People with higher incomes have more opportunities to fulfil their material wishes. They can afford more goods and services. At the same time, they enjoy a higher social status. The relationship between income and subjective well-being has been the object of extensive empirical research. The results are clear: People with higher income unambiguously consider themselves to be more satisfied with their lives than do persons with low income. The glory sometimes attributed to poverty, for instance as a consequence of a natural life without stress, turns out to be a romantic myth. As the expressionist artist Willem de Kooning rightly remarked: "The trouble with being poor is that it takes up all your time"; the poor incessantly have to think of money. With low material resources, additional income strongly raises life satisfaction. But once a certain level of affluence is reached, additional income only has a weak influence on average happiness. Rich people's life satisfaction rises only little when their incomes further increase. It is not possible to indicate an exact income level beyond which happiness barely rises any more. It depends very much on the economic and social environment one lives in, as well as on personality characteristics.

Somewhat surprisingly, people who mainly pursue idealistic goals are happier than those concerned with material goals, and who take financial success and social recognition as points of comparison.

The results gained for economically advanced countries also apply to people in developing countries, where a poor person's happiness rises even more strongly with additional income.

The relationship between income and happiness is characterized by decreasing marginal utility. There is a positive, but increasingly weak relationship; other influences on well-being, such as having good social relationships and good health, begin to dominate. There are even situations where additional income is felt to be a burden. This applies to some winners of large lotteries. At the beginning, life satisfaction certainly rises. But the winners sometimes give up their jobs. They thus lose important personal relationships and recognition; they often feel that other people are only interested in them because they now have a lot of money. Relatives and friends expect to be financially supported. According to their own evaluation, the average life satisfaction of lottery winners after an adjustment period does not prove to be significantly higher than before winning.

What applies to income groups also holds for countries as a whole. Higher average income is associated with higher subjective life satisfaction. People living in rich countries are on average considerably happier than those who live in poor countries, even taking into account the different costs of living.

This relationship between income and happiness is not only revealed in econometric studies that hold other determinants of happiness constant but also in the raw data, as shown in Chap. 2. The inhabitants of rich countries, such as Norway, Denmark, Iceland, Finland, Sweden, Switzerland and the Netherlands, are the happiest, while people living in poor developing countries, such as Central African Republic, Burundi, Tanzania, Rwanda and Togo, are considerably less happy.

Work

People who lose their jobs are much more dissatisfied with their lives than are those who hold jobs. In one sense, this result is surprising because, as explained above, as an experiment income is kept constant, and only the isolated effect of having no work on happiness is considered. Thus, people with the same income but without work are much less happy than those who have to work for their income. The reasons for the strongly negative effect of unemployment on happiness lie in sociological and psychological factors. People without work lose their self-confidence and feel excluded from the rest of society, which is largely composed of employed people. Unemployed people living in a region with many other unemployed therefore feel less unhappy than those living in regions in which most people are employed.

If unemployment rises in a country, not only the unemployed suffer but also other parts of the population. Employed people are less happy because higher unemployment is accompanied by greater economic and financial uncertainty, which may threaten their own jobs. Moreover, high and rising unemployment may lead to unwelcome social unrest.

What also matters for life satisfaction is the kind of job one does. People who have considerable autonomy in their work, that is, who can largely determine themselves how to act, are more satisfied with life than those working under a strict hierarchy. This is the reason why the self-employed are happier. On average self-employed persons work harder and longer hours, have to cope with more risk, and have lower incomes than those working in organizations. What makes them more satisfied with their lives is the measure of autonomy they enjoy. For the same reason, independent artists are happier than people subject to directives and orders from above.

Distribution of Income

The inequality of income between people has a remarkable influence on happiness. Inhabitants of the United States differ in their evaluation from Europeans. Americans believe that they live in the country with the greatest opportunities and therefore do not feel negatively affected by rising inequality in income; they are neither happier nor unhappier. Higher income is taken as an indicator that hard work and initiative are profitable and lead to greater rewards. Americans believe that they may benefit in the same way in the future. In contrast, Europeans are convinced that upward mobility is restricted and that they are therefore unlikely to gain a much higher income in the future. However, actual upward mobility is not very different on the two continents; if anything, more people move upward from a lower to a higher income group in Europe. It is subjective evaluations and ideologies that determine how the level and change in income distribution affects happiness.

Economic Development

The relationship between the development of national income, or Gross National Product (GNP), and subjective well-being has been analysed in depth for many individuals and groups of countries. The results are astonishing. Despite the strong increase in material wealth, a ground-breaking study for the United States did not find that average life satisfaction increased over time. This is surprising (it is called the Easterlin Paradox after its author) because cross-section analyses between individuals have clearly established that higher income raises happiness. The paradox can be explained by the fact that over time people become accustomed to higher income; after some time; they take it more or less for granted.

Another explanation is that people always tend to compare themselves to people with higher incomes. This seems to be an innate trait of human beings, and it has helped us to raise our material well-being from extreme poverty to today's wealth. If people compare themselves to others, a rising national income pushing up the income of all no longer contributes to individual happiness.

This result has been questioned in several careful analyses. For countries other than the United States, such as Japan, Italy, and various other Western European countries, average happiness increases with rising GNP. The exact relationship between individual well-being and national income needs to be explored further. There is no doubt that human happiness does not rise linearly with material prosperity. Economic growth raises life satisfaction, but the additional contribution to happiness increasingly vanishes.

Socio-Demographic Influences

Age

Research has established a clear U-shaped relationship between age and life satisfaction, assuming health remains constant. Young people are especially happy, because they believe that they can achieve everything in their lives. In the middle years, people become less happy, because they become aware that not everything can be achieved. Moreover, they are under considerable pressure to have a successful career and at the same time to have a good family life. With increasing age, people become happier, because they have learnt not to try to achieve the impossible. They endeavour to enjoy what they have, which contributes to their life satisfaction.

Family Status

Married people are happier than those living alone and even than those living in unmarried partnerships. Those who are married are less oppressed by loneliness; marriage or a stable partnership to some extent provides a counterweight to the stress of work life.

Children

On average, children do not contribute to happiness, as they require enormous attention, good nerves, and money, and they make it more difficult to engage in activities such as sports or visiting arts events. As soon as children have grown up and left home, their parents are happier than those without children. In turn, grandchildren are a source of happiness for grandparents.

Social Relationships

Intensive and regular social contacts within the family and among friends and acquaintances contribute strongly to happiness. This is one of the most well-established results of well-being research.

Health

Health is one of the most important contributors to well-being. This is true for both physical and psychological health. Subjectively perceived good health and subjective life satisfaction are closely related. Health evaluated objectively by medical doctors, in contrast is less strongly correlated with life satisfaction. This is because different people deal in differing ways with their health status. People who are ill or who suffer an accident seem to cope relatively well with their situation. They often compare themselves to individuals who are in even worse health.

Psychological illness is a major contributor to unhappiness.

Education

A more advanced education opens more opportunities in life and is conducive to happiness. In particular, leisure time activities can be pursued in a more active and diversified manner.

Culture and Religion

Subjective well-being differs considerably between countries and cultures. In the United States, there is strong social pressure to call oneself happy; people acknowledging that they do not feel happy are not appreciated. In contrast, in France a person stating that he or she is happy is considered weird and suspected of missing human depth. This is well reflected by French philosophers, especially the existentialists, who emphasized the tragedies in the world, and who considered happiness to be a superficial phenomenon. This view is also prominent beyond left-wing philosophers. President Charles De Gaulle is said to have uttered: "Only idiots are happy". This attitude also applies to Italians and to some extent also to Germans, who coined the term *Weltschmerz*, which has entered several other languages.

Religious people have been shown to be happier than those who do not belong to a religious community. People believing and trusting in a higher being are better able to cope with the adversities of life. A negative event in life can be given a higher reason, thus helping to balance one's state of mind. At the same time, engagement in a religious community leads to more intensive human contacts and relationships; these work against isolation, which decreases happiness. As already pointed out, intensive social contacts within the family and among friends and acquaintances contribute strongly to happiness.

Political Conditions

Democracy and Well-Being

Institutional conditions and political systems are a major determinant of human happiness. Research has established that economic activity fares better in democratic rather than authoritarian societies. Happiness research goes further and inquires whether these factors also raise the subjective well-being of the people living in a country. In this context, it is important to consider two mutually enforcing causal relationships. On the one hand, democratic conditions make people happier; on the other hand, happy citizens are more likely to support a democratic political system.

The positive influence of democracy on happiness is due to two factors:

- Political decisions correspond more closely to the wishes or preferences of the citizens. The politicians are induced by the need to be re-elected to supply the public services and to promulgate the regulations desired by the population.
- Individuals cherish the chance of participating in political decisions as such, quite independent of the outcomes. This dependence of happiness on the way outcomes are achieved has been called "procedural utility". The positive relationship between democracy and life satisfaction corresponds to the fundamental psychological quest for self-determination.

The importance of democracy for subjective life satisfaction has been demonstrated by cross-section analyses for a large number of countries. The more extensively democratic the political institutions are, the happier are people living under them.

The same result is obtained for the different options for political participation in the 26 Swiss cantons. In cantons in which the citizens have greater opportunities to directly participate in political decisions via popular initiatives and referendums, people are more satisfied with their lives than in cantons where the direct participation rights of citizens are less extensive (where, for instance, fiscal aspects such as tax rates and public expenditures are excluded).

The positive relationship between the extent of democracy and subjective well-being is stronger for Swiss citizens than for foreigners living in Switzerland. The latter benefit in roughly the same way from improved political decisions but may not participate in political decision-making. The Swiss derive satisfaction from being able to engage in politics; they enjoy a measure of procedural utility. It is worth remembering that the observed differences in life satisfaction take into account all other determinants of happiness. The observed differences in subjective well-being between cantons with differing participation chances is therefore not due to other factors such as higher or lower income, or a different age structure of the citizenry.

Federalism

The subjective life satisfaction of citizens is also higher the more political decisions are taken at a local level. They feel that their wishes are taken more seriously than if they were considered at a distant centre. Local supply of public goods and services takes better into account the different geographic, cultural, religious, social, and economic preferences of the population. Local political decisions are better able to observe and follow many of the population's wishes.

Literature

The literature cited in Chap. 1 of this text discusses the various factors quantitative research has found to systematically influence life satisfaction.

The empirically based insight that increasing income does not necessarily raise happiness is due to:

Easterlin, Richard A. 1973. Does Money Buy Happiness? *The Public Interest* 30: 3–10.

Easterlin, Richard A. 2010. *Happiness, Growth, and the Life Cycle*. New York: Oxford University Press.

The following article reaches a somewhat different conclusion:

Stevenson, Betsey, and Justin Wolfers. 2008. Economic Growth and Subjective Well-Being: Reassessing the Easterlin Paradox. *Brookings Papers on Economic Activity* 39 (1): 1–87.

The political and institutional aspects determining happiness are developed in:

Frey, Bruno S., and Alois Stutzer. 2000. Happiness. *Economy and Institutions. Economic Journal* 110 (446): 918–938.

Veenhoven, Ruut. 2000. *Conditions of Happiness*. Dordrecht, Boston, Lancaster: Reidel.

Chapter 4
Consequences of Happiness

Abstract Happiness has various effects: Persons considering themselves to be happy act differently in many life circumstances. Happier persons are more productive, in better health, and therefore live longer. The positive consequences of happiness are illustrated using the case of health. The effects can be captured by various methods: A large number of persons are observed over many years; emotions can be manipulated in laboratory experiments; and the impact on health of personal misfortunes such as the loss of a marital partner can be explored. Often it is difficult to establish in which direction the relationship between cause and effect works. To identify the direction, lottery winners are analysed. This analysis shows that higher income and wealth indeed raise happiness, though only for a short period.

The Importance of Several Joint Influences

How important are the various determinants of subjective well-being? The results of happiness research clearly indicate that the private sphere is as important as the public domain. Thus, both work and leisure strongly determine people's happiness. Individuals derive satisfaction not only from income but also from work and social relationships. Self-determination and the opportunity to use one's own competencies are a precondition for engaging in activities providing happiness. In addition, the process by which the results are reached also provides satisfaction. This is well expressed by the saying that "the journey is the reward".

The most important aspects of life providing happiness are satisfying work, a good material living standard, family and friends, leisure, and health. The everyday elements of life are central to our subjective well-being. As has been pointed out, political participation rights also impact our well-being. The absence of wars, terrorism, and civil war are other crucial requirements for a happy life.

B. S. Frey, *Economics of Happiness*, SpringerBriefs in Economics,
https://doi.org/10.1007/978-3-319-75807-7_4

The Effects of Happiness

People considering themselves to be happy act differently in many life circumstances. Happier people are more successful on the job market. The more satisfied that people are with their lives, the more willing they are to work hard. Such people work more intensively, with greater engagement, and are more creative; this leads to a higher per-capita income for individuals and the country as a whole.

A positive correlation is also obtained for the marriage market. It is easier for happier people to find an attractive partner, and they are less lonely. Happier people are more cooperative and more inclined to help others.

The positive consequences of happiness are illustrated using the case of health:

Happy people are in better health and live longer. Voltaire (1694–1778) quipped: "J'ai decidé d'être heureux parce que c'est bon pour ma santé" (I have decided to be happy because it's good for my health).

However, the positive effects on health of happiness are not simply a fairy tale. This relationship between subjective well-being, physical health, and life expectancy has been carefully analysed in many studies.

Happiness has been measured in a number of different ways, most importantly with long-run and evaluative subjective life satisfaction, but also using short-term positive emotions such as joy and laughing and negative emotions such as grief and fear.

Happy individuals enjoy longer lives; almost fifteen per cent longer than that of people considering themselves to be unhappy. In industrial countries, this means that happy individuals can expect to live around ten years longer than unhappy ones. Happy people are also less likely to commit suicide. Comparing happiness to other well-known influences on health, such as smoking or obesity, the influence of life satisfaction on health and longevity is pronounced.

How can the impact of happiness on physical health and life expectancy be captured? Several notable methods are available. The most important are the following:

- A large number of individuals are observed over many years whether they are happier and indeed healthier and live longer than other people. One well-known instance of this is termed the "nun study". Before young women join a religious order and enter a monastery, they are asked to indicate their happiness level. It turns out that those nuns who considered themselves to be happier before entering the monastery lived longer than those who stated that they were less happy. Nuns are particularly well suited for such studies because they spend their lives under very similar conditions.
- Emotions can be manipulated in laboratory experiments, for example by showing participants cheerful and sad pictures. The influence of particular physiological factors whose effect on health is well known can thus be explored.
- The effects on happiness and health of events produced by nature such as tempests or floods can be analysed. For example, one day after the major 1994 earthquake

in Los Angeles, mortality in the city was five times higher than it was in the weeks before the event.

- Finally, the impact on health of personal misfortune such as the loss of a marital partner can be explored. A study has, for example, shown that the mortality of men who lost their wives in the first month of grief is twice as high as under normal circumstances. With women whose marriage partner has died, the respective mortality rate is three times as high.

Studies demonstrate that high subjective life satisfaction and positive emotions contribute to better health and to a longer life. But care must be taken not to associate happiness with all kinds of illness. In particular, given the present state of knowledge, it may not be convincingly argued that happiness helps to reduce metastatic cancer.

Empirical studies also find consequences of eudaimonic well-being on health and length of life. There are protective health benefits, in particular in coping with the challenges of growing old. Interestingly, eudaimonia also buffers against inequality; people deal with it in a more philosophical way.

Causality

Often it is difficult to establish in which direction the relationship between cause and effect works. For instance, it is not obvious whether married people become happier or happy people find it easier to get married. The same applies to work: Are employed people happier or is it easier for happy persons to find a job because they are more active, innovative and open? The same factors can be both determinants and consequences of subjective well-being.

To answer these questions, it is helpful to consider a specific case, namely lottery winners. Winning a lottery can be considered an exogenous event independent of the participant. Therefore, the lottery win can be taken to a cause, while the change in subjective life satisfaction can be considered a consequence. Lottery winners indeed state in the following year that they are happier. This allows us to conclude that higher income and wealth raise happiness, though only for a short time period. Income produces subjective well-being, most importantly in poor countries below a certain level of living.

Literature

Diener, Ed, Sarah D. Pressman, John Hunter and Desiree Delgadillo-Chase. 2017. If, Why, and When Subjective Well-Being Influences Health, and Future Needed Research. *Applied Psychology: Health and Well-Being* 9 (2): 133–167.

Oswald, Andrew J., Eugenio Proto, and Daniel Sgroi. 2015. Happiness and Productivity. *Journal of Labor Economics* 33 (4): 789–822.

Chapter 5
Psychological Influences on Happiness

Abstract Individual happiness is to some extent constructed by the individuals themselves and depends on the past and present social environment. Many individuals adapt quite quickly to a new situation and move towards a similar well-being level as they experienced before a positive or negative event. However, this is not always the case. Our well-being depends not so much on absolute income but on our income compared to colleagues, friends, and relatives. This also holds for unemployment. Experiments reveal that people are incapable of accurately remembering the pain they experienced in the past. Wrong decisions are often taken because people disregard the scale and speed of adjustment to a new situation. Human beings tend to be overoptimistic and find it difficult to predict how happy they will be in the future under different life circumstances.

Happiness Is Partly Self-constructed

Subjective well-being has both affective and cognitive aspects. The cognitive components comprise the rational and intellectual aspects of happiness and involve evaluations and comparisons. Happiness is not simply given but is subjective. To some extent, it is constructed by the individuals themselves and depends on the past and present social environment. In particular, the following mechanisms and processes must be taken into account.

Adaptation

What happens if a person experiences an unexpected positive or negative event?

Consider a large lottery win or a grave accident. In the case of the lottery win, happiness first rises markedly but thereafter falls quite quickly. In the case of a grave accident, a similar adjustment takes place, but in the reverse direction. At first, well-being falls strongly, but after some time most people fortunately are able to deal with

B. S. Frey, *Economics of Happiness*, SpringerBriefs in Economics,
https://doi.org/10.1007/978-3-319-75807-7_5

the new situation, and their happiness level rises again. Many persons adapt quite quickly and move towards a similar well-being level as they experienced before the accident. However, this is not always the case. For instance, employees who are dismissed are markedly less happy than before and remain so after a considerable number of years.

Comparison with Other People and Situations

The evaluation of our happiness is not absolute; it is determined by comparisons with peer groups and persons, as well with one's own situation in the past. Our well-being depends not so much on absolute income as on our income relative to colleagues, friends and relatives. This also holds for unemployment. People without work are less happy than those employed, but they are less unhappy when they live in an environment in which many other persons are without work. The reference groups are not strictly determined. Most people choose a comparison group materially better off. This is surprising, because people would be better off comparing themselves to people who are in a less fortunate situation.

Cognitive Biases

There are circumstances and conditions in which it is impossible, or at least very difficult, to raise one's happiness level. Experiments reveal that people are incapable of accurately recalling the pain they experienced in the past. What is remembered is the pain suffered at the end of the experiment as well as the maximum pain. They do not remember the duration over which they experienced pain. As a consequence, human beings tend to take wrong decisions when they have a choice of maximum pain and pain at the end or how long they have to experience the pain.

Wrong decisions are often taken because people disregard the size and speed of adjustment to a new situation. Many people want to gain higher and higher income, only to experience thereafter that they become used to it and that the additional income affects their well-being level only moderately or even not at all. Such a cognitive bias leads to a stress of wanting to continually raise one's income.

Human beings tend to be overoptimistic. Most assume that their future personal situation is superior to those of other people. For example, they underestimate the probability of being involved in an accident or of being affected by cancer or Aids. Most people overestimate their own capacities. A large majority of car drivers believes, for instance, that they are better than the average driver—which is of course impossible. Successes tend to be attributed to one's own effort and knowledge, while failures are attributed to external forces.

Restricted Prognostic Abilities

Human beings are incapable of predicting how happy they will be in the future under different life circumstances. When they consider their future well-being, they are strongly moved by hopes and expectations. If they can fulfil them, they are satisfied with their lives. Most people underestimate the speed with which they adapt to new conditions. They find it difficult, if not impossible, to take this adjustment process into consideration. As a result, their choices are biased.

Careful analyses of major changes in life circumstances such as life shocks in the domain of social relationships (widowhood, unemployment and disability) and in life decisions (marriage, separation and divorce) suggest that people make substantial prediction errors with respect to the life satisfaction they will actually experience in the future. The discrepancy between self-predicted and actual satisfaction is greatest with respect to widowhood. People are overly pessimistic regarding their recovery from widowhood. The same holds for experiencing unemployment and disability. The reason is that people have biased beliefs about future changes in circumstances, but above all they underestimate how quickly and strongly they are able to adapt to these unfortunate changes in life. For marriage, in contrast, people tend to be overly optimistic about their actual life satisfaction after five years.

When comparing alternatives, material factors are weighted more heavily than non-material ones. The future happiness produced by ideal components is underweighted. We dedicate too little time to our families, friends, and hobbies. In contrast, we overestimate material aspects such as income or status. Such mistaken evaluations have been shown to exist for the case of commuting. People are prepared to suffer long travel times to raise their income or to have particularly attractive living conditions in their homes. However, surveys on well-being have shown that subjective happiness is, ceteris paribus, lower the longer time commuting requires.

Literature

Frey, Bruno S., and Alois Stutzer. 2014. Economic Consequences of Mispredicting Utility. *Journal of Happiness Studies* 15 (4): 937–956.
Kahneman, Daniel. 2011. *Thinking, Fast and Slow*. New York: Farrar, Straus and Giroux.
Stutzer, Alois. 2004. The Role of Income Aspirations in Individual Happiness. *Journal of Economic Behavior & Organization* 54 (1): 89–109.

A recent study on self-predicting future life satisfaction is:
Odermatt, Reto and Alois Stutzer. 2018. (Mis-)Predicted Subjective Well-Being Following Life Events. *Journal of the European Economic Association*, forthcoming.

Chapter 6
Happiness Maximization by the Government

Abstract Fundamental arguments speak against politicians attempting to maximize the aggregate subjective well-being index of their country's population. This approach to economic policy corresponds to the idea of a "benevolent dictator" who determines from above what is good for the people. Such an assumption is naïve. Once the maximization of the aggregate happiness index of the population is taken to be the official goal of economic and social policy, one can no longer trust that survey respondents answer any questions about their subjective life satisfaction in an unbiased way. When citizens' happiness is taken as the measuring rod of politics, government politicians will make an effort to manipulate the aggregate happiness index in their favour. For both these reasons, the subjective well-being data are no longer a reliable measure of people's happiness. Governments should not be asked to maximize happiness.

Should Politicians Maximize Happiness?

From the results gained by happiness research, some authors conclude that politicians should aim to maximize the happiness of their populations. Politicians are thus asked to directly employ the insights of happiness research to raise the aggregate subjective well-being index as much as possible. This would fulfil the dream of putting the Theory of Quantitative Economic Policy into action. According to this theory, the state should maximize the social welfare function. As self-reported subjective well-being is a close proxy to social welfare, it is now possible to specify the objective function to be maximized. Happiness research now supposedly provides the empirical tools to proceed in that manner.

At first sight, this goal appears to make sense. After all, it seems evident that to maximize the happiness of people is a better goal than to maximize gross national income or the trade surplus. However, fundamental and convincing arguments speak against this approach to economic policy. Aiming to maximize social welfare corresponds to the idea of a "benevolent dictator", who determines from above what is good for his or her people. Politicians are assumed to undertake only those policies

B. S. Frey, *Economics of Happiness*, SpringerBriefs in Economics,
https://doi.org/10.1007/978-3-319-75807-7_6

which are beneficial to society. Such an assumption is naïve. It is more reasonable, and much better confirmed empirically, that politicians' main goal is to stay in power. In democratic countries, politicians must win elections to stay in power. To reach that goal, they employ all the means available, even sometimes illegitimate and illegal ones. In particular, unpopular measures, such as reducing a budget deficit or accumulating funds to be able to cover future old age pensions, are shifted to the future when these politicians are no longer in power and no longer responsible. Politicians are quite ready to raise their popularity with voters by offering election gifts such as hand-outs and subsidies. Such political behaviour contradicts the long-run interests of the population but is either not fully observed or strongly discounted by those who directly benefit from the monetary and non-financial hand-outs given by the politicians in power. Only when the individuals in government are convinced that they can win the forthcoming election do they undertake policies according to their own convictions. But these may be ideologically laden and do not necessarily conform to the wishes of the citizens.

Biased Answers to Happiness Surveys

Once the maximization of the aggregate happiness index of the population is taken to be the official goal of economic and social policy, as has long been the case in Bhutan, followed by France, the United Kingdom, Germany, and Australia, one can no longer trust that the survey respondents answer the question about their subjective life satisfaction in an unbiased way. The results of happiness research are ideally based on surveys in which the respondents report in an uninfluenced way how happy they feel they are. But if the respondents are aware that their answers are used for political purposes, they will change their behaviour and take into account the political consequences. People for instance, who hold conservative views are likely to answer that they are particularly happy when a conservative party is in power. Conversely, they are inclined to punish a left-wing party in power by stating that they are less happy than they are in actual fact. Such behaviour undermines the validity of surveys and hampers the empirical basis of happiness research.

Manipulated Happiness Index

When citizens' happiness is taken as the measuring rod of politics, government politicians will make an effort to manipulate the aggregate happiness index in their favour. As this index is the result of representative surveys, there are many opportunities to do so. People who are critical of the government or who are considered outsiders can be excluded from the population surveyed. For instance, inmates of jails can be disregarded, because they are unlikely to be satisfied with their lives. In some countries, such as the United States, this follows the legal norms according to which prison inmates have no voting rights. In the same vein, people indicating a particularly low life satisfaction (e.g. those indicating below 4 on a scale of 10) can be taken to be "unreliable" and therefore excluded from the aggregate happiness index. If such manipulations do not suffice to jack up the aggregate happiness index sufficiently, the government can shift responsibility to uncontrollable events such as natural disasters or influences from foreign countries. As a result, the government can argue that the aggregate happiness index must be corrected. This is in line with the corrections of the inflation index that many governments undertake when an uncontrollable exogenous price rise occurs.

As the survey respondents answer in a biased way, and governments will manipulate the subjective well-being data, a government's happiness maximizing policy is likely to produce an unreliable measure of people's happiness. The data become seriously misleading both for policy purposes and for empirical research. It follows that governments should *not* be asked to maximize happiness.

Literature

Frey, Bruno S., and Alois Stutzer. 2012. The Use of Happiness Research for Public Policy. *Social Choice and Welfare* 38 (4): 659–674.

Chapter 7
What Happiness Policy Is Appropriate?

Abstract Happiness may not be the only goal of human beings. Personal development, virtue, fairness, companionship, freedom, and solidarity may also matter. The political process should provide everybody the opportunity to find his or her own way to reach happiness. At the constitutional level, citizens appreciate increased political participation rights in the form of popular initiatives and referendums in which issues of content are decided. They prefer a federal political organization in which local units have extensive decision rights about both expenditures and taxes. In current politics, citizens can urge politicians and public officials to follow the insights gained in happiness research. Important areas include, for instance, the job market and economic growth, income inequality, independence, voluntary work and donations, social relationships, education, and liveable cities. Politicians can discuss the proposals with the population, and if supported, put them into practice.

Enabling Happiness

The previous Chap. 6 argues that a government should not aim to maximize the aggregate happiness index directly; this would correspond to a paternalistic or even dictatorial policy that would be incompatible with democratic principles. Rather, the political process should provide every person the opportunity to find his or her own way to reach happiness. The insights of happiness research make an important contribution to reach this goal. They help to improve economic and social policy such that people become more satisfied with their lives.

Happiness as Ultimate Goal?

Engaging in a happiness policy first involves considering whether happiness really is the only goal of human beings. It may well be that happiness is merely one ingredient of a good life. Personal development, virtue, and fairness may also be

B. S. Frey, *Economics of Happiness*, SpringerBriefs in Economics,
https://doi.org/10.1007/978-3-319-75807-7_7

important. Other people may put companionship, freedom, and solidarity on the same level as subjective happiness. Other ultimate goals may be physical and social well-being. Other people rank factors such as trust, self-regard, absence of pain, work satisfaction, and satisfaction with one's family and partnership alongside happiness. Liberal thinkers value personal freedom higher than happiness. They even emphasize the productive effects of unhappiness. They suggest that dissatisfaction with one's life is a goal to aim for and a motor to achieve, ever more. From the point of view of evolution, it is not happiness that matters but survival and reproduction.

A further distinction considers not only the goal but also the path to the goal. Processes leading to happiness may also contribute to life satisfaction. Most people are happy if they master a challenging activity. When people devote themselves fully to an activity, they forget time and space, and they experience a "flow of life".

Happiness policy must take into account the kind of subjective well-being that is to be sought. This decision can only be taken on the basis of philosophical and religious considerations and must be left to the individual persons. If happiness in the form of eudaimonia is taken as the ultimate goal of human beings, as argued by Aristotle, different consequences follow than when only momentary happiness is to be achieved. Modern, quantitatively oriented happiness research focuses on the life satisfaction reported by individuals. This evaluation of one's own well-being is cognitive and considers a life as a whole. It takes into account experienced, expected, and remembered happiness.

Institutions Leading to Happiness

A reasonable happiness policy should focus primarily on constructing and maintaining institutions that allow people to reach their own goals of happiness in the context of the society they live in. Written and unwritten constitutions determine the formal and informal institutions whose political and social processes guide human beings to achieving their own happiness. Decisions about the fundamental structure of the political system must be taken behind the veil of uncertainty, so that no one knows the situation in which he or she or the descendants will be in the future: rich or poor, well or little educated, healthy or sick. This uncertainty prevents decision-makers from establishing institutions to their own benefit. In contrast, dictators regularly impose new constitutions on their population to suit themselves (e.g. allowing themselves an unrestricted number of years in power).

Happiness research contributes important insights that help identify the institutions that support the subjective well-being of individuals. Most importantly, it has been shown that citizens value the opportunity to participate in political decisions. They appreciate participation rights in the form of popular initiatives and referendums in which issues of content are decided. Such possibilities at regional and national levels have been discussed in many countries but should also play a larger role in new political units such as the European Union.

Happiness research also shows that citizens prefer a federal political organization in which local units have extensive decision rights concerning both expenditures and taxes. Local councils and even smaller units such as urban districts should have more competencies.

In addition to established political corporations, new units can also be considered. One such proposal is that of *Functional, Overlapping and Competing Jurisdictions* (FOCJ). They are established to address problems. In contrast, historically existing political corporations normally have territorial extensions often as a result of pure chance. Examples of such problems are the provision of water, schools, public security, transport and other infrastructural buildings, and trade relations. The political unit for each function is to be formed in an appropriate territorial jurisdiction based on democratic principles. In contrast to the technocratic functional units that exist in some countries, FOCJ respond to the wishes of the population. The citizens elect the executives of the functional units and may intervene directly via popular initiatives. Important decisions require approval by compulsory popular referendums. As the territorial extensions of FOCJ differ, they overlap. Some functions can be addressed at a very local level while other functions, such as free trade and defence, are best dealt with at a supranational level. Individuals or local councils may freely choose which FOCUS (this being the singular of FOCJ) they wish to enter. A crucial prerequisite is that each jurisdiction is free to set its own tax rates so that it obtains the revenues with which to fulfil its services to the community. As a result, the FOCUS has a strong incentive to manage both taxes and expenditures in a responsible way.

Today, no such FOCUS exists in a pure form, but in many countries, in particular in the United States and in Switzerland, precursors exist in one form or other; however, there is still a long way to go before they are broadly established. Not surprisingly, many politicians and bureaucrats in traditional political units strongly oppose these new governmental units, as they promise to function more efficiently and more democratically. Under the regime of FOCJ, the national state is able to survive only if it is able to fulfil a particular function in a better way than newly established FOCJ. But what could these functions be? For free trade or defence, the national state tends to be too small—here a more extensive political unit such as NATO is more appropriate. For other functions such as education or crime prevention, it is too large. FOCJ promise to raise people's subjective well-being as they combine democratic responsiveness with economic efficiency.

Institutional changes should in no case be promulgated in an authoritarian way by the government. Rather, new forms of political decision-making should emerge from a discourse that includes as many citizens as possible. Such a procedure may be based on aleatoric elements, or selection by lot. This method of political governance was extensively and successfully used for many hundreds of years in classical Athens, in the flourishing medieval Italian city-states of Venice, Siena, and Genoa, and in Swiss communes. A number of citizens are elected randomly from the overall population and asked to participate in small groups to discuss a particular issue and to propose a policy. The parliament must then decide about the various proposals and put them to voluntary or obligatory referendums, in the case of important changes, as described by law. The members of parliament can be elected in the traditional way, but this method results in a highly skewed representation of income and educational groups. It is well known that present parliaments are composed mainly of people with higher than average income and education. In many cases, it may therefore be preferable to have two houses of parliament, one elected in the traditional way, another composed by random selection, to ensure that all groups in society are well represented.

Increased participation rights can also be introduced into organizations beyond the state. In modern societies, people want to have more intensive and effective participation rights, from which today they are excluded in many places. In a large number of public organizations, individuals have little or any participation rights. Examples are mighty sports organizations and media houses, which partly benefit from and act in the realm of public support. The same holds for international organizations such as the International Labour Office (ILO), the North Atlantic Treaty Organization (NATO), and the European Union.

A particular issue is the participation rights of workers in corporations. In Germany, this has been extensively introduced and imposed from above. Happiness research supports another avenue. Happy workers are more involved, productive, creative, and in better health. This insight should induce firms in their own interest to give their employees more autonomy, thus raising their self-esteem and feeling of competence.

Happiness in the Current Politico-Economic Process

In politics, the current "rules of the game" are enshrined in the constitution. The citizens can make suggestions that insights gained in happiness research are taken into account and followed by politicians and public officials. Conversely, politicians in government or in the opposition can take up proposals derived from happiness research, discuss them with the population, and if supported, put them into practice. The politicians are induced to follow this line as they can expect an advantage in the competition for votes. The results of well-being research presented above open many possibilities. Here, only a few particularly relevant aspects are discussed.

Job Market and Economic Growth

Unemployment strongly reduces the level of happiness of those people directly affected as well as for the rest of society. A government should therefore prioritize combatting unemployment. What is most important is the reduction of joblessness among young workers, because individuals once put out of work or never having been employed are negatively affected, or "scarred", for all their lives. In comparison, economic growth should be emphasized less, because the adaptation processes in many cases do not sustainably raise the happiness level.

Income Inequality

Differences in status produced by income can be considered a zero-sum game. When one person earns more than others and thus increases his or her status, the status of others is automatically reduced. Society as a whole does not win. The results of happiness research, however, suggest that in most countries large income differences between people reduce the overall happiness level of the population. For this reason, a common suggestion is to impose high tax rates on high-income recipients to achieve a more equal income distribution. However, there are important arguments against this proposal:

- High taxation of upper income recipients tends to produce negative incentive effects. Some of the most productive members of society are induced to work less or to shift their activity into the hidden or shadow economy. The allocation of resources is biased to the disadvantage of the whole population.
- Competition for status may well be an inherent, genetically given trait of human beings. If this is the case, they will emphasize other factors producing status than highly taxed income. Some of these may be positive, in particular when there is a status competition in education. No harm is done with a competition for titles and awards. If, however, status competition is undertaken by amassing political power, it may well have negative effects. The other members of society also lose when the status competition involves having as much leisure as possible and undertaking activities such as spending whole days or even weeks playing golf. This seems to have been true for the English and French upper class. An equally negative status competition is one in which clothes emphasize the differences between individuals in the social hierarchy. This is the case for monarchic and military societies such as Germany between 1870 and 1918.

These are some of the reasons why it is not necessarily a good idea to impose high taxes on the rich to quell status competition. It may well be that the people living in such societies feel less satisfied than before.

The effect on happiness of income distribution existing at a particular point of time also depends on the opportunity of people to move upwards. An individual who earns a low income over a restricted period of time but sees a chance to move up the income ladder in the future is less unhappy than an individual who feels trapped in his or her income position. Indeed, people who are confident that they will be able to leave a low-income position may even welcome a large spread in incomes. Empirical research suggests that many Americans adhere to this dream and therefore are not unhappier when the distribution of income in the populations widens. In fact, however, this is only a dream as the mobility between income recipients is not larger in the United States than in European countries.

Independence and Self-employment

Many persons aspire to achieve a position of independent work rather than having to tolerate pressures and orders in a corporate hierarchy. They do that even though they may well be aware that on average income is lower than when working in a firm and that they have to work harder and with more risk. The political process should therefore make a great effort to reduce the bureaucratic impediments to founding companies and to entering self-employed work. At the same time, training should be offered in becoming independent.

Voluntary Work and Donations

Doing good for others raises one's own happiness. Therefore, more opportunities should be offered to enable people to be active in charitable organizations, for instance by providing insurance when they work on their behalf. Equally, donations should be favoured.

Even more importantly, help and care for the old and sick within families and outside should be supported. This would not only relieve the state but also contribute to the well-being of the people engaged. Such activities can be honoured by bequeathing awards and orders, provided they are handed out in a serious way, to signal the specific voluntary contribution to society a person has made.

Family and Social Relationships

The more intensive the social contacts among people are, the happier they feel. The family provides stability and intimacy and should not be subject to higher taxation than is the case for unmarried partners. This is still the case in some countries. When two people work and their income is added because they are married, tax progressivity leads to their total income being taxed to a higher extent. As a consequence, founding a family is punished.

Clubs and the church also contribute to subjective well-being provided they do not isolate themselves but are open to outsiders. What matters is not so much financial support for such organizations but encouragement and publicity from government.

Education

The better people are educated, the more they can develop their capacities, and the more satisfied they are with the lives they lead. It is particularly important to support those groups in society who up to now have had little chance to acquire a more advanced education. The government should strongly foster the dual learning systems in which young persons gain practical experience in the workplace and in schools learn more general abilities such as languages and methods of successfully engaging in the market. Offering opportunities to acquire a more advanced education at later stages in life is bound to raise the life satisfaction of many people.

Liveable Cities

The happiness of people can also be raised by constructing and changing cities so that they enable and induce close personal contacts among inhabitants. In this respect, urban planning over the years has contributed greatly to raising the subjective well-being of city dwellers. The dominance of soulless huge apartment buildings and the dominance of car traffic have given way to cities focusing on the needs of their inhabitants. The elegance of buildings has been combined with roads and squares meeting the relational desires of people. In former times, the beauty of buildings was the dominant goal of architects and city planners, the capital city Brasilia being a negative example.

The topics discussed in this section provide examples only how the political process can indirectly contribute to the human happiness. There are many other areas in society, in which careful public interventions can potentially improve life satisfaction while leaving people the freedom to find and choose their own way to happiness.

Literature

Alesina, Alberto, Rafael Di Tella, and Robert MacCulloch. 2004. Inequality and Happiness: Are Europeans and Americans Different? *Journal of Public Economics* 88 (9–10): 2009–2042.

Csikszentmihalyi, Mihaly. 2014. *Flow and the Foundations of Positive Psychology: The Collected Works of Mihaly Csikszentmihalyi*. Dordrecht: Springer.

Frey, Bruno S., and Reiner Eichenberger. 1999. *The New Democratic Federalism for Europe: Functional Overlapping and Competing Jurisdictions*. Cheltenham, UK: Edward Elgar.

Chapter 8
What About a Happiness Pill?

Abstract Happiness pills provided by the government free of charge would have several positive, but also negative consequences. The procedural aspects of happiness are important and should not be neglected. Politicians may have an incentive to keep the population quiet by offering them happiness pills for free. But this may backfire if citizens are then induced to engage more strongly in political activities against the wishes of politicians. It is illusory to expect that happiness pills are able to raise people's well-being over an extended period of time.

Happiness Pills Exist

Today, many people consume drugs quite similar to what could be called "happiness pills". These are not only individuals for whom doctors have prescribed pills to overcome depression and other psychological illnesses. A considerable number of people routinely take pills to raise their happiness level. Prozac is the best-known product, but many other pills produce similar effects. "Brain doping" is widely practised; the substances consumed are related to amphetamines, which raise the concentration of dopamine in the brain. A considerable number of people consume illegal drugs. And for a long time, a substantial share of the population in all countries has sought to push up their well-being by consuming alcohol, tobacco, tea, and coffee. According to this broad definition, only a small proportion of people do not consume any substances to raise their feeling of happiness. Huxley's *Brave New World* with its *soma* is not far away.

A Thought Experiment

Assume that a happiness pill exists that has no negative effects on the health of the people consuming it, and that its use does not produce any psychological or physical addiction. Moreover, assume that the government distributes the happiness pill free

B. S. Frey, *Economics of Happiness*, SpringerBriefs in Economics,
https://doi.org/10.1007/978-3-319-75807-7_8

of charge. These conditions mirror an extreme situation and do not reflect today's reality. However, it may well be possible that pharmaceutical research will be able to provide such a pill in the future. This goal may be called "bio-happiness". It may also be possible that in the future some governments will offer the happiness pill to its population without cost.

Nevertheless, most people are likely to reject such an offer, for intuitive reasons. The results of several surveys suggest that a large proportion of the population would not consume a happiness pill, even if they were to receive it free of charge. For example, Australians were asked the following question: "If there was a legally available drug that could be bought over the counter, that made you feel happy, and did not have any side-effects, do you think there would be occasions when you would take it? Would you say: Yes, definitely; Yes, probably; No, probably not; No, definitely not; Don't know". This was the result of the survey: Three quarters of the respondents said they would not consume a legally available happiness pill.

Positive Effects

Continuing with the thought experiment, consuming the happiness pill raises its consumers' subjective hedonic feelings of happiness. Empirical happiness research indicates that the happier people are, the more successful they are at work, the more friendly is their behaviour towards others, and the more optimistic they are. Moreover, they are in better health and live longer.

The positive mood produced by the happiness pill also corrects the genetic inequality regarding the possibility to experience happiness. As Chap. 3 pointed out, the extent to which individuals can experience happiness depends quite strongly on the genetic endowment they inherited from their ancestors. Between fifty and eighty per cent of the happiness feeling has been attributed to this "genetic lottery", so it is of substantial importance when considering differences in happiness between individuals.

In addition to the direct effects of the happiness pill on its consumers, it is also necessary to look at its consequences for people who do not take it:

- Happiness is contagious. Happy people also make other people happier;
- A higher level of happiness supports friendship, loyalty, pro-social behaviour, and solidarity.

These two effects of the happiness pill also improve the situation of people who do not take it. They constitute a classic positive external effect. It can thus be argued that the distribution of happiness pills to potential consumers should be subsidized because it also raises the well-being of other people.

Negative Effects

The consumption of happiness pills may also have noxious consequences on other people. The most important of these is the negative effect on work motivation. The incentive to work diminishes or even disappears completely because happiness is solely produced by the consumption of the pill. Its consumers no longer perceive any need to work. Engaging in work only occurs for intrinsic reasons: because someone likes to work or because a social norm has been internalized. Reliance solely on these motivations cannot be sustainable from an economic perspective. People taking the happiness pill need nourishment and accommodation and would like to enjoy the many other positive aspects of modern life. It would be pure fluke if the existing intrinsic motivation and social norms led to exactly the supply of goods and services people desired. Some of these goods and services will be provided by the consumers of happiness pills who are intrinsically motivated. This may well be the case, for instance, with respect to the arts and culture. In contrast, it is unlikely that essential goods and services such as the construction of houses and the cleaning of streets and toilets will be supplied in the amounts required.

It follows that the happiness pill undermines an economy in which people depend on goods and services whose production requires hard work and effort. This observation constitutes an important counterargument against a general distribution of happiness pills to the population.

Substitutes and Complements

A supply of happiness pills free of charge reduces the demand for illegal drugs such as cocaine and heroin. As they are quite costly and risky to obtain, and moreover affect the health of their consumers negatively, it might be expected that their demand disappears almost completely. This constitutes a positive external effect, because illegal drug production and distribution are major causes of crime. As a result, the cost of police and prisons is drastically reduced, and people feel more secure.

However, today's experience with drug use suggests that a considerable share of consumers will exhibit a strong inclination to take the happiness pill in addition to illegal drugs. As such additional consumption still takes place under illegal conditions, it is dangerous and involves crime. If this is the case, the free supply of the happiness pill may well reduce aggregate happiness, because the addiction to drugs persists.

As the thought experiment so far has not been put into reality, it is open whether the introduction of freely available happiness pills actually would promote a substitutive or complementary effect. For reasons of caution, it is important to take the complementary effect seriously.

Procedural Benefits

Evaluating whether the happiness level of the consumers of happiness pills really rises also requires consideration of another important aspect. Individuals not only value the level of income or the number of good friends they have. They are not solely hedonistically oriented. They also put great value on the process by which happiness is attained. People are happier if they attain a goal by their own effort rather than if it just happens to them. An example is the effort expended to reach the peak of a difficult mountain. When reaching the top, the climbers are satisfied and happy. The higher the effort needed, the happier they are. Consuming a happiness pill does not provide any procedural utility and therefore leads to lower satisfaction. In the extreme, the well-being of an individual may even fall.

The Paradox of Happiness

Happiness cannot be consciously sought but is a side-product of a life that involves meaningful activities and human relationships. Nobody can just decide to be happy; it is ridiculous to believe that. If someone tries to attain happiness in this way, it disappears. This phenomenon is well known and was emphasized long ago by philosophers such as Plato and Aristotle. According to this paradox, it is impossible to reach happiness with the help of a pill in the long run, because such consumption is unrelated to a good and meaningful life.

For similar reasons, it is impossible to maintain a high happiness level over an extended period of time. Happiness can only be appreciated when this condition can be compared to less happy situations.

The search for happiness through consuming pills is basically mistaken.

Selfish Governments

The concept of a happiness pill is based on the assumption that governments are both able and willing to pursue and raise people's happiness. Our thought experiment assumes that the government can indeed provide a happiness pill without harming the health of the people consuming it. The crucial question therefore is whether governments have the intention to pursue such a policy.

Theoretical and empirical research in modern political economy has come to the clear conclusion that this is not the case. The politicians in power are interested in pursuing quite different goals: they want to act in their own interests. As individuals, politicians also value income and the recognition by others. At the same time, they belong to a specific group of people for whom exerting power over others is particularly important. What matters is how these goals are connected to the welfare of the population. Only in an ideal democracy with a strong and continuous competition between parties are politicians obliged to carefully observe the wishes of the voters. These conditions rarely occur. In fact, today's world is still characterized by dictatorships and authoritarian governments whose political leaders do not follow the preferences of the population.

It could be argued that politicians have an incentive to keep the population quiet by offering them happiness pills at no charge. This view assumes that happy people would interfere less—or not at all—in politics than if they were less happy. In this case, politicians distributing the happiness pill would indeed have the opportunity to act freely according to their own wishes. Such a situation corresponds to Huxley's soma in his novel *Brave New World*. This soothing drug turns its consumers into totally passive human beings.

Research into happiness suggests that the contrary is true. Happier people tend to be more active and enterprising. Consuming happiness pills might even induce citizens to engage more strongly in political activities, which may be incompatible with the goals of politicians. People in government risk losing their uniquely powerful positions. This view has a long history. Ever since democracy was instituted in Athens and other classical Greek city-states, it has been argued that when the citizens are happy and little constrained by material concerns, they engage in politics. If this is indeed the case, politicians have little incentive to provide the population with happiness pills free of charge.

What Can Be Said?

This chapter does not claim that a happiness pill exists which has no noxious effects on consumers' health. However, it can well be imagined that a pill with these properties may become available in the future. To some extent, we already observe an extensive use of substances that are supposed to raise their consumers' subjectively experienced happiness.

There would be some remarkable positive consequences of freely available happiness pills. The consumers would be nicer, act in a more pro-social manner, enjoy better health, and live longer as the genetic lottery responsible for a considerable proportion of happiness is changed in their favour. People would be able to turn to superior cultural and political goals. But there would be grievous negative consequences of providing happiness pills; in particular it would not be possible to maintain an economy providing the goods and services people need and want to consume. Most importantly, the procedural aspect of happiness is totally neglected. Only what is achieved by some measure of one's own effort and devotion contributes to long-run well-being.

Considering these positive and negative aspects of providing a happiness pill leads to the conclusion that it is illusory to expect that such a policy is able to raise the people's well-being in a sustainable way.

Literature

The conditions and effects of soma are discussed in the famous novel by:
Huxley, Aldous. 1932. *Brave New World*. New York: Harper & Brothers.

The term "genetic lottery" is used by:
Walker, Mark. 2011. Happy-People-Pills for All. *International Journal of Wellbeing* 1 (1): 127–148.

This article also discusses various aspects of the supply of happiness pills. See also:
Katolik, Aleksandra, and Andrew J. Oswald. 2017. Antidepressants for Economists and Business School Researchers: An Introduction and Review. *Die Unternehmung* 71 (4): 448–463.
Martin, Mike W. 2008. Paradoxes of Happiness. *Journal of Happiness Studies* 9 (2): 171–184.

That happy people live longer is shown in:
Diener, Ed, and Micaela Y. Chan. 2011. Happy People Live Longer: Subjective Well-Being Contributes to Health and Longevity. *Applied Psychology: Health and Well-Being* 3 (1): 1–43.

The importance of procedural utility for well-being is analysed by:
Frey, Bruno S., Matthias Benz, and Alois Stutzer. 2004. Introducing Procedural Utility: Not Only What, But Also How Matters. *Journal of Institutional and Theoretical Economics* 160 (3): 377–401.

The role of effort as an important ingredient of happiness is explored by:
Loewenstein, George. 1999. Because It Is There: The Challenge of Mountaineering... for Utility Theory. *Kyklos* 52 (3): 315–343.

Models of governments' and politicians' behaviour are presented in:
Mueller, Dennis C. 2003. *Public Choice III*. Cambridge: Cambridge University Press.

Chapter 9
Happiness and Consumption

Abstract Standard economics assumes consumers to be rational actors, but happiness research suggests that consumers tend to mispredict the utility of activities and that they face self-control problems. People often hold incorrect intuitive theories about the determinants of happiness. They overestimate the impact of specific life events on their experienced future well-being with regard to both intensity and duration. There are four major sources for the systematic over- and undervaluation of choice options: the underestimation of adaptation, distorted memory of past experiences, the rationalization of decisions, and false intuitive theories about the sources of future utility.

Welfare Judgments

Conventional economic theory assumes that people are perfectly rational. They are fully informed about how much utility they gain from consumption; this is revealed by what goods and services they demand. Individuals are also capable of maximizing their utility. According to this theory, people do not make any systematic mistakes when making consumption decisions; if they occurred, individuals would correct them in the long run by learning.

In contrast, subjective well-being surveys reveal the welfare judgments of individuals. Retrospective evaluations are taken as a valuable source of information about the bounded rationality in people's decision-making. How do people fare after they have made decisions? This is particularly relevant if people have limited self-control.

Limited Self-control and Individual Well-Being

In standard economics, people have no self-control problems. They are able to make decisions according to their long-term desires. From this point of view, consuming goods and pursuing activities that some people consider addictive, or at least forming

B. S. Frey, *Economics of Happiness*, SpringerBriefs in Economics,
https://doi.org/10.1007/978-3-319-75807-7_9

bad habits, such as smoking cigarettes, taking cocaine or watching TV extensively, are considered a rational act. In contrast to this view, many people judge their own and other people's consumption behaviour as irrational. They think that they would be better off if they consumed less of these goods and cared more for their future well-being. The standard approach in economics does not allow us to differentiate between the view of consumers as rational actors and consumers mispredicting utility or facing self-control problems. However, with a proxy measure for individual welfare at hand—subjective life satisfaction—competing theories can be discriminated.

Misprediction of Utility

Standard economics assumes that people can successfully predict utility. However, happiness research has actually studied whether people are indeed successful in forecasting the utility they are about to experience. It turns out that people accurately predict whether an emotional experience primarily elicits good or bad feelings. However, they often hold incorrect intuitive theories about the determinants of happiness. For instance, they overestimate the impact of specific life events on their experienced well-being with regard to both intensity and duration.

The standard economic model of consumer decisions is probably appropriate for most goods and activities and for most situations. However, there are situations in which people have to decide between different activities, goods or options, which differ systematically in the extent to which their future utility can be correctly predicted. If this is the case, systematic negative economic consequences emerge. Some options, or attributes of options, are more salient than others when making a decision; these are relatively overvalued. If people choose options according to this evaluation, their experienced utility is lower than what they expected. It is also lower than what they could have experienced if they had not mispredicted their utility. Moreover, they consume different goods with different attributes and pursue different activities than in a situation where no option in the choice set would have special salience.

Four major sources of the systematic over- and undervaluation of choice options can be distinguished:

- the underestimation of adaptation,
- the distorted memory of past experiences,
- the rationalization of decisions, and
- false intuitive theories about the sources of future utility.

Underestimated adaptation to new situations has become part of models of intertemporal decision-making. They include the misguided purchase of durable goods and consumption profiles with too much consumption early on in life.

It has often been argued that the work-life balance of individuals today is distorted. People are induced to work too much and to disregard other aspects of life. This has been proposed most forcefully for the United States, where individuals are said to be "overworked". This is a misprediction of utility: people overvalue income relative to leisure because income is often more salient. Competing for status involves negative externalities and therefore too much effort is invested in gaining status and acquiring "positional goods". These are goods which act as status symbols, signaling their owners' high relative standing within society. Mispredicting utility magnifies the distortions of competing for status in consumption if utility from consumption is overvalued.

Mispredicting utility might also explain people's behaviour in courts of law. When it comes to making decisions, individuals tend to prefer institutions that promise favourable outcomes. But afterwards, they state that they would have preferred the institution to place more emphasis on fair procedures. This finding suggests that people tend to overvalue outcome relative to procedural utility.

People's decisions to commute for a longer or a shorter time also relates to the misprediction of utility. The commuting decision involves a trade-off between the salary and the quality of housing on the one hand and commuting time on the other hand. Rational utility maximizers commute only when they are fully compensated by higher salary and better living conditions. However, when people overestimate utility from goods serving extrinsic wants, they opt for too much commuting and so suffer lower well-being. An extensive study in Germany found that commuting is not fully compensated, and that, on average, people who commute twenty-two minutes each way (sample mean) would need an additional thirty-five per cent of their monthly wage income to be as satisfied with their life as people who do not commute. They make a decision that lowers their self-declared life satisfaction.

When people make trade-offs, material factors attract more attention than intangible factors such as friendship. Consumption of material goods is overvalued due to the neglect of adaptation, rationalization, and memory biases. As a result, material goods are over-consumed and individual well-being is reduced compared to situations in which people mispredict utility less.

Literature

Parts of this chapter are based on pp. 695–701 in:

Stutzer, Alois, and Bruno S. Frey. 2010. Recent Advances in the Economics of Individual Subjective Well-Being. *Social Research* 77 (2): 679–714.

Fundamental aspects of human decision-making are treated in:

Kahneman, Daniel, and Richard Thaler. 2006. Anomalies: Utility Maximization and Experienced Utility. *Journal of Economic Perspectives* 20 (1): 221–234.

Particular aspects of consumption and happiness are discussed in:

Stutzer, Alois, and Bruno S. Frey. 2008. Stress that Doesn't Pay: The Commuting Paradox. *Scandinavian Journal of Economics* 110 (2): 339–366.

Stutzer, Alois, and Armando N. Meier. 2016. Limited Self-control, Obesity, and the Loss of Happiness. *Health Economics* 25 (11): 1409–1424.

Chapter 10
Happiness and Television Viewing

Abstract Watching TV is a major human activity. Many people are tempted to watch television rather than to pursue more engaging activities. Individuals with incomplete control over their own behaviour watch more TV than they consider optimal for themselves. Their well-being is lower than they could achieve. Heavy TV viewers, and in particular those who lose a great deal of time that might have been spent doing something else, report lower life satisfaction. Long TV hours are also linked to higher material aspirations and anxiety.

An Important Consumption Activity

Watching television today is one of the most important leisure activities for most people in most countries. People in Europe spend almost four hours per day viewing TV. This average varies considerably between countries. While only about ten per cent of people in Switzerland watch television more than three hours a day, more than thirty-eight per cent do so in Greece. In the United States, people spend more than five hours per day, on average, in front of their television sets. In many countries, watching TV occupies almost as much time as working.

Subjective time use data are often criticized as being inaccurate or biased. "Watching television" might not be understood in the same way by all respondents, and they might not differentiate between television viewing as a primary, secondary, or even tertiary activity. Respondents might not even correctly remember all the times they watched television, or they might revert to social norms or to images they would like to have of themselves. Nevertheless, answers to such questions seem generally to be a reliable measure for television viewing behaviour.

As watching television is a totally voluntary, freely chosen activity, it seems obvious that people enjoy it, because they would not do it otherwise. This implication is shared by standard neoclassical economic theory. Individuals are assumed to know best what provides them with utility. They choose the amount of TV consumption that provides them with most utility. However, recent developments, particularly in behavioural economics, have cast doubt on this conclusion. In general, it is not possi-

B. S. Frey, *Economics of Happiness*, SpringerBriefs in Economics,
https://doi.org/10.1007/978-3-319-75807-7_10

ble to infer the utility by simply observing a particular behaviour, because individuals do not always act rationally. People may also be subject to habits over which they do not have full control. They may consume some goods, such as drugs, alcohol, or tobacco, to a greater extent than they find to be good for themselves. They suffer from a self-control problem. One consequence of this is that, according to their own evaluation, smokers consider themselves to be better off if smoking is restricted by a tax. Happiness research has shown empirically that individuals overestimate the utility of future income at the same time as they underestimate the benefits of interacting with other people. The consumption decisions made by individuals are systematically distorted according to their own evaluations.

People suffering a self-control problem are mainly induced to watch too much television because it offers immediate benefits—entertainment and relaxation—at very low immediate marginal costs. Many costs, such as not having enough sleep and underinvesting in social contacts, education, and career, are experienced only in the future. People with time-inconsistent preferences are therefore unable to adhere to the amount of TV viewing they planned or which they would consider optimal for themselves in retrospect. Extensive TV consumption, consequently leads to a lower level of individual utility than could be achieved.

Effects of Television Watching on Happiness

Data on subjective well-being can be used to study whether people make systematic mistakes in their choice of the amount of time they devote to TV watching. The following empirical analysis considers data from more than 42,000 individuals in 22 different countries in the period 2002/03.

The econometric estimate lends support to the hypothesis of over-consumption. Controlling for all other influences, excessive TV viewers report lower life satisfaction. People who are subject to time constraints but still watch TV for many hours are particularly affected by lower life satisfaction.

There is ample evidence that individuals may suffer self-control problems with television consumption. Some forty per cent of adults and seventy per cent of teenagers in the United States admit that they watch too much TV. Short- and long-term evaluations of TV consumption tend to diverge. Many people state that they do not enjoy television in general, but consider the programmes they saw last night to be pretty good.

Some individuals abstain from watching television totally, because they know that they would otherwise not be able to control their viewing behaviour. They cancel their subscription for cable TV to avoid "zapping" too much, lock their TV set away in a cupboard, or place an uncomfortable chair in front of it.

People who watch less than half an hour of TV a day are more satisfied with their lives than people who consume any other level of TV time. For those watching TV for anything between half an hour and two and a half hours, average reported life satisfaction is lower than in the group of people watching for less than half an hour.

The negative effect is even larger for people watching for more than two and a half hour a day.

These findings suggest that extensive TV watching makes people worse off, because it indicates overconsumption due to a self-control problem and misprediction of future costs.

The size of the effect of TV consumption on happiness can be compared to other influences on happiness. For example, the difference in life satisfaction between those watching more than two and a half hours and those watching less than half an hour is more than one third of the difference in life satisfaction between people who are with a partner and those without. The difference is about the same as that between people with upper secondary education and those who only completed primary school or the first stage of basic education.

Effects Differ Between Groups

The correlation between TV consumption and life satisfaction is estimated for the whole population and thus represents an average effect of TV viewing across individuals. However, self-control problems in television consumption do not affect everybody in the same way. It is most likely that some groups of people suffer higher disutility from extensive TV consumption than others.

People who can use time more profitably when not watching TV are said to have higher opportunity costs of time. This includes the self-employed, for instance craftsmen, lawyers, architects, and artists. The same applies to individuals in high positions such as managers, top bureaucrats, and politicians. These people can freely transfer time from leisure to work. For these groups of individuals, the self-control problem of watching too much TV generates considerable costs. Their happiness is drastically lowered if they are unable to fully control themselves. In contrast, people with a great deal of time available, such as the unemployed and the retired, suffer little if any disutility when they fail to watch the amount of TV they would consider optimal for themselves. TV consumption significantly lowers the life satisfaction of individuals with high opportunity costs of time, while it has a smaller negative effect on the life satisfaction of individuals with low opportunity costs of time.

The negative correlation of television consumption and subjective well-being has been interpreted as over-consumption leading to a lower happiness level. However, this correlation could well be the result of reverse causation: it is quite plausible that unhappy people watch more TV than happy ones.

Literature

The relationship of television viewing and happiness is treated in:

Bruni, Luigino, and Luca Stanca. 2006. Income Aspirations, Television and Happiness: Evidence from the World Values Survey. *Kyklos* 59 (2): 209–225.

Some of the evidence presented in this chapter is taken from:

Frey, Bruno S., Christine Benesch, and Alois Stutzer. 2007. Does Watching TV Make Us Happy? *Journal of Economic Psychology* 28 (3): 283–313.

The broader context of television watching as a social activity is discussed by:

Corneo, Giacomo. 2005. Work and Television. *European Journal of Political Economy* 21 (1): 99–113.

Kubey, Robert, and Mihaly Csikszentmihalyi. 1990. *Television and the Quality of Life. How Viewing Shapes Everyday Experience.* Hillsdale, NJ: Lawrence Erlbaum.

A fascinating case of time inconsistency and the problem of self-control is the subject of:

DellaVigna, Stefano, and Ulrike Malmendier. 2006. Paying Not to Go to the Gym. *American Economic Review* 96 (3): 694–719.

Chapter 11
Happiness and Management

Abstract Happy people have higher intrinsic motivation to work, which raises their productivity. Some firms exploit happiness to attract more customers. Such business policy exploits happiness in an instrumental way; this flies in the face of true happiness. In what kind of happiness can business organizations engage? A firm should offer all its stakeholders the possibility to achieve happiness. Firms should create a work atmosphere that supports employees' autonomy and creativity and foster valuable social relationships. Individuals can then pursue their quest for happiness in the way best for themselves.

Effects of Happiness on Business Activities

Life satisfaction has strong effects on activities and conditions relevant for business. These are the most important impacts in this context:

- Happy people are more interested in the work they perform and are more engaged, thus raising their productivity. In contrast, unhappy people do not like their work and tend to be careless, which affects their work output negatively. These results have been found in laboratory experiments that carefully control for other influences. In one experiment, some randomly chosen subjects' happiness levels were manipulated by showing them a cheerful picture, while those in the control group were not. Treated subjects had twelve per cent greater productivity in a subsequent piece-rate task compensated by money. They increased their output but not per-piece quality of work. To check this effect, major unhappiness shocks experienced in real life—bereavement and family illness—were analysed. The results confirm those of the laboratory experiment.
- Happy people have higher intrinsic motivation to engage in work, appreciate more autonomy, and are more creative, which again contributes to better work.
- People professing to have high life satisfaction are less affected by contagious deceases and are healthier. Good health contributes substantially to more effective work. Unhealthy workers impose substantial costs on firms even in a well-developed social security system.

B. S. Frey, *Economics of Happiness*, SpringerBriefs in Economics,
https://doi.org/10.1007/978-3-319-75807-7_11

- People satisfied with the life they lead are less inclined to engage in strikes, rebellions, and outright civil war than are people who feel unhappy. Happiness tends to deter crime. The absence of these disturbing political and social conditions helps business to fulfil its role.

Instrumental Use of Happiness

Mostly in American firms, but also elsewhere, there is a trend to exploit happiness so as to attract and retain more customers. In the United States, there is a consultancy called Delivering Happiness; it has a Chief Happiness Officer (CHO), a global happiness navigator, and a happiness alchemist. The idea is to induce employees to create "happiness hygiene". Employees are expected and strongly induced to smile as they work and show other expressions of positive emotions. This tendency is especially prominent in the service sector, whose importance in the economy has been rising in recent decades. Accordingly, some firms make an effort to create happiness with their staff by offering them courses on mindfulness and yoga lessons.

Such a business policy in which happiness is exploited in an instrumental way flies in the face of happiness as used in the economic research discussed here. Subjective well-being must reflect the unbiased and unconstrained feelings of a representative selection of individuals. This is obviously not the case if employees are forced to look and behave in a happy way. If the employee behind the counter in a McDonalds shop appears to be happy when serving hamburgers, few customers believe that such demeanour reflects a true feeling. Rather, most of them know that it is a marketing technique and nothing more.

Various Forms of Happiness

But what about "true" happiness produced by business organizations? Here the question arises what a "firm" means in this context. There are at least four possible ways to answer this question:

- The happiness of *managers*. While this may in many cases be actual policy, it is normatively unacceptable that only the well-being of the executives is considered.
- The happiness of the *employees*. This would again be a complete misunderstanding of the function of a firm. A firm should certainly not exclusively care for employees' well-being—though this may be true in reality in some cases—but it should provide goods and services that the market demands.
- The happiness of the *owners* of firms. Again, this is a wrong target because dividends and other streams of money compensate the owners of firms.
- The happiness of the *stakeholders* consisting of all the people that have relations with the firm, including suppliers, customers, and other people affected in various

ways by a firm, such as having to bear the burden of noise or environmental exhausts.

Many people, including some scholars, would argue that maximizing the happiness of stakeholders is desirable. However, more careful considerations suggest that this is unwarranted. There are four major reasons why stakeholder happiness maximization should not be attempted:

- The weighting given to the various groups is an arbitrary decision. Should the happiness of barely affected suppliers have the same weight as that of full-time employees who spend a considerable part of their lives within the firm? Depending on what weights are chosen, any overall happiness measure can be constructed for the firm as a whole.
- The executives of a firm can at best guess what makes their stakeholders happy, but they do not really know. In any case, the respective persons know better, and in a free society should have the right to decide for themselves rather than have the decision made for them.
- When people are asked about their life satisfaction but know, or suspect, that it is used to measure the happiness of a firm, they are likely to answer in a different way than is the case under conditions where the respondents answer in a more truthful way because their answers are not given instrumentally.
- Managers of firms whose happiness is to be evaluated can easily manipulate the corresponding happiness index. They can simply delete answers reporting low happiness, for instance by deleting those individuals from the vaguely defined group of stakeholders. At the same time, they can increase the number of high happiness answers, for instance by inducing and cajoling their employees to supply such answers, or by hiring "very happy" people for low part-time jobs and only for the period in which the surveys are undertaken.

Offering Possibilities for Happiness

These considerations suggest that it is a mistaken idea to try to maximize the happiness of a firm. What a firm can and should do is to offer its stakeholders opportunities to achieve happiness. Most importantly, firms should create a work atmosphere conducive to employee satisfaction, which should support their own thinking and creativity and foster valuable social relationships. Bequeathing awards are a useful procedure to support desirable behaviour. In addition, work should not be so demanding and burdensome that employees are unable to enjoy their leisure time. The income provided should be sufficient to lead a good life with respect to material standards. The length of commuting time should be reduced as far as possible, for example by offering more flexible work hours.

In addition, happiness research considers the general role of firms in society. They should offer good value for money and should abstain from deceiving consumers by providing false or misleading information. A notable recent case of this occurred in the German car industry with respect to the environmental damage produced by diesel engines. Such deception has direct consequences for people's well-being: Empirical research shows that inhabitants of Germany who suffered a reduction in air quality through noxious emissions report a reduction in subjective life satisfaction.

Achieving these and other goals in the best possible way requires high managerial capabilities, but it means that the individuals that have contact with the firm can pursue their quest for happiness in the way best for themselves.

Managers can benefit from the knowledge gained of the determinants and perhaps even more of the consequences of subjective well-being. However, they should not engage directly in trying to raise the happiness of their employees, suppliers, customers, and other stakeholders. Rather, they should lay the ground for these people to be able to reach happiness in the way they choose themselves.

Literature

Parts of this chapter follow:

Frey, Bruno S. 2017. Research on Well-Being: Determinants, Effects, and its Relevance for Management. *Die Unternehmung* 71 (4): 358–367.

Effects of happiness important for management are analysed in:

Fisher, Cynthia D. 2010. Happiness at Work. *International Journal of Management Reviews* 12 (4): 384–412.

Oswald, Andrew J., Eugenio Proto, and Daniel Sgroi. 2015. Happiness and Productivity. *Journal of Labor Economics* 33 (4): 789–822.

Yuan, Leo. 2015. The Happier One Is, the More Creative One Becomes: An Investigation on Inspirational Positive Emotions from Both Subjective Well-Being and Satisfaction at Work. *Psychology* 6 (3): 201–209.

Despite its title, the following collection of articles almost exclusively deals with various aspects of job satisfaction:

Cooper, Cary L., and Ivan T. Robertson. 2013. *Management and Happiness*. Cheltenham, UK, Northampton, MA, USA: Edward Elgar.

Possibilities to induce desired behaviour in firms and beyond are presented in:

Frey, Bruno S., and Jana Gallus. 2017. *Honours versus Money. The Economics of Awards*. Oxford: Oxford University Press.

Chapter 12
Happiness and Religion

Abstract Modern happiness research makes it possible to empirically measure the impact of religion on subjective well-being. There is a positive correlation between religion and happiness, with a robust effect of churchgoing and Protestant confession, while the results regarding internal religiosity or faith are more ambiguous.

Models of Religious Activity

Economic models seek to explain religious activity and individual choice of denomination. Individuals are assumed to allocate time and goods between religious and consumer goods in such a way as to maximize the sum of utility from the present life and the afterlife. Through regular religious activities, a "religious asset" is accumulated in the present life. The religious asset will be consumed in the afterlife, with utility resulting from it. Calculating the opportunity cost of acquiring the religious asset can explain some of the existing empirical patterns. Thus, as women and retired people receive lower incomes on average, they are more likely to spend time in church, since their opportunity cost of going to church is smaller than for people with higher income.

There are various payoffs to religious activities that individuals can earn in this life. The benefits gained immediately and derived from religion include, among others, a sense of purpose or meaning, group identity, and social support. There is also a learning process that is related to religion. Individuals accumulate religious capital by regularly exercising religious rites. In other words, they acquire human capital, which enables them to execute religious activities more efficiently and at decreasing costs. Higher human capital leads to higher benefits from religious activity. Religion can be seen as a learning-by-doing process. The more experience one has, the less demanding is the maintenance of faith; these individuals are said to enjoy a decreasing marginal cost of faith. This dynamic helps to explain the greater religiosity of elderly people. Religious human capital increases with age, leading to lower cost of faith and a higher optimal level of faith.

B. S. Frey, *Economics of Happiness*, SpringerBriefs in Economics,
https://doi.org/10.1007/978-3-319-75807-7_12

Types of Religiosity

Religion can be divided into internal and external religiosity. Internal religiosity or faith is defined as belief in God and a trusting acceptance of God's will. External religiosity refers to all observable activities that are undertaken in a religious context, most conspicuously when going to church. It is useful to distinguish between these two dimensions, since subjective well-being can be affected by both or either of them, and they might work in different ways. For example, it is not clear whether church attendance increases subjective well-being by proximity to God and the lessons learnt during the service or because one has social contacts with other churchgoers.

Internal Religiosity: Faith

Researchers have established a positive relationship between faith and subjective well-being: believing in God has a positive impact on global happiness, life satisfaction, life excitement, and marital happiness. Religious people also suffer from fewer negative psychological consequences of traumatic life events. It has even been found that no other factor influences life satisfaction more than does religious belief.

Several reasons have been proposed to explain the clear positive connection between faith and subjective well-being. Individuals may derive happiness from a relationship with a supernatural being with whom they interact. In addition, belief in God enables individuals to create a system of meaning and thus greater purpose in life. Through religion, setbacks in life can be understood as part of a greater plan and as a challenge. This explanation is supported by findings in psychology where the handling of personal setbacks with faith, termed religious coping, has a significant impact on well-being.

Internal religiosity or faith creates spillover effects to non-religious people. People are more satisfied with their lives in more religious regions, and this holds both for those who are religious and for those who are not.

The overwhelming evidence of a positive impact of internal religiosity on happiness has to be interpreted cautiously: Most of the studies concentrate on the United States, where more than ninety per cent of the population describe themselves as religious and where religiosity plays a pronounced role even in modern life. Results in less religious countries, such as Denmark or the Netherlands, do not show such clear evidence of an effect of faith on happiness.

External Religiosity: Attending Church Service

Going to church and building social networks within one's religious community plays an important role for religious individuals. Studies have shown that the frequency of church attendance increases the probability of reporting greater happiness. It also has a significant positive impact on marital happiness. Church attendance has a higher impact on happiness than praying. Analogous to the spillover effect of internal religiosity, church attendance also has positive spillovers on the well-being of others at the aggregate level.

The impact of church services on well-being is related to the community life they engender. Church life is an important factor in religion and its effect on subjective well-being. It is not religious service attendance per se that has an impact on well-being, but the number of friends in one's congregation. Happiness derived from religion is thus only partly caused by proximity to God; friends in the church community are also responsible for the increase in happiness. People can gain greater happiness by having a close network of friends without necessarily being religious.

Denomination

Happiness researchers have also investigated whether reported well-being differs depending on one's denomination. Such a hypothesis is justified given the differing value systems and institutional structures of churches. Protestants have been found to be happier than Catholics. This effect is explained by the organizational structure of these denominations: Protestants derive greater well-being from a higher autonomy in their belief, from their collective identity, and from better social integration. Moreover, Christians in general seem to have an advantage compared to other religions in subjective well-being. The probability of being happier is considerably higher for pious Christians than for Buddhists. However, some studies do not find any impact of denomination on well-being in Europe.

Religiosity can also have an indirect effect on happiness. Most religious rules promote a healthy lifestyle and communicate values and norms that facilitate and strengthen social connections. Religious people also serve more often as volunteers, which is associated with higher subjective well-being.

Effect Size

Going to church is positively correlated with subjective well-being in a statistically significant way. This finding is in line with other findings that attribute the positive correlation to the effects of social networks, social contact, and group identity. Compared to other factors influencing happiness, this correlation is quite strong. Going to church at least once a week substantially increases happiness. The effect on happiness is of a similar magnitude as having a partner instead of being single. It is also sizeable compared to the most important factor in happiness estimations, having a job compared to being unemployed.

Literature

A survey on the economics of religion is provided by:

Iannaccone, Lawrence R. 1998. Introduction to the Economics of Religion. *Journal of Economic Literature* 36 (3): 1465–1495.

An important early contribution to the relationship between religion and happiness is given in:

Pollner, Melvin. 1989. Divine Relations, Social Relations, and Well-Being. *Journal of Health and Social Behavior* 30 (1): 92–104.

Econometric analyses are offered by:

Clark, Andrew E., and Orsolya Lelkes. 2009. Let Us Pray: Religious Interactions in Life Satisfaction. PSE Working Papers 2009-01.

Greene, Kenneth V., and Bong Joon Yoon. 2004. Religiosity, Economics and Life Satisfaction. *Review of Social Economy* 62 (2): 245–261.

Steiner, Lasse, Lisa Leinert, and Bruno S. Frey. 2010. Economics, Religion and Happiness. *Zeitschrift für Wirtschafts- und Unternehmensethik* 11 (1): 9–24.

Chapter 13
Happiness and War

Abstract A crucial question of happiness research is how people who died in military conflicts should be treated. The present procedure of surveying the living does not consider the potential future happiness of the deceased. Alternatively, the well-being lost by the people who died in a war can be calculated. There are some benefits of war to individuals such as feelings of solidarity, mutual support, and national pride, as well as "combat flow". There may also be an "afterglow" that glorifies the combat experience. Research results indicate a substantial loss in well-being due to terrorist incidents.

Fundamentals

One of the great open questions in well-being research is how people's well-being is affected by military and social conflict. The readers may be surprised that this is even considered an issue at all. It may appear completely obvious that wars make people drastically unhappy. However, such a conclusion is less straightforward than appears at first sight.

A major problem to be considered is how people who die in war should be treated in empirical happiness research. There are, of course, other reasons for death, such as malnutrition, natural disasters, and crime, to which similar issues apply as those considered here. One related issue arises when part of the population of a country is deported and is then no longer counted among the inhabitants. This was the case, for instance, in the Kingdom of Bhutan, which substituted Gross National Product with Gross National Happiness. However, it evicted a considerable number of inhabitants of Nepalese ethnicity from its territory, an aspect disregarded in the calculations of Gross National Happiness.

This chapter focuses on the deadly effects of wars to highlight the fundamental issues at stake. The basic problem can best be understood by considering the following cases.

B. S. Frey, *Economics of Happiness*, SpringerBriefs in Economics,
https://doi.org/10.1007/978-3-319-75807-7_13

- A person, take a male soldier, is badly wounded during a war. His happiness will therefore strongly decrease. He may recover after some time but will not reach the same level of well-being previously enjoyed. Even if his recovery is full, there is still a period in which the person experiences a drastic loss of well-being. The happiness indicator for that particular country is therefore lower than it would be without this war incident.
- Compare the situation of the wounded soldier to another person, say a female civilian, who dies during a war. She disappears from the living and cannot be asked about her level of life satisfaction. Her happiness is totally neglected, even though the fate of dying is in most cases worse than surviving, even if gravely wounded. The deceased person does not directly lower the aggregate happiness indicator of the country, because she is not counted. However, there can be an indirect effect due to the mourning of relatives and friends.

The difference made in the calculation of happiness between the two situations is striking: the worse situation, that of a person dying, is reflected by a higher aggregate happiness indicator than the relatively better situation in which the person survives.

How can this problem be solved? Two solutions come to mind. The first endeavours to calculate the *happiness lost* by the influence of the war. The second seeks to solve the dilemma by definition, by excluding the dead. Only the happiness of the living is counted.

The research results discussed here are revealing but incomplete: little systematic and empirically compelling evidence is available on how military conflict affects individual well-being. Happiness researchers are reluctant to deal with the effect of war activities on happiness for several reasons. Firstly, there is a serious data problem. Normally, no surveys are undertaken in times of war to capture how happy or satisfied people are with their lives. Secondly, there are many types of military conflicts with many different outcomes. Thirdly, there are also many indirect consequences of wars. For example, during military conflicts the health condition of the population decreases, lowering its aggregate well-being. The influenza epidemic that broke out during and after the First World War killed more people than perished in combat in that war. Finally, democratic rights in wars are usually curtailed, and authoritarian decision-makers take over. While failing democracy is known to reduce happiness, it may be argued that the conditions in war differ from periods of peace. Even well-established democracies often resort to more authoritarian rules in times of war.

Causality may not only run from war events to well-being, but also from well-being to war events if, for example, unhappy individuals are more inclined to support conflict resolution by military means. The strength of the two directions of causality can only be isolated if good data (in particular panel data) are available, which is not generally the case for military conflicts and well-being.

The Well-Being Lost by the Dead

The well-being a person would have enjoyed had he or she survived a military conflict can be calculated from econometric estimates of individual happiness. These show the determinants of individual life satisfaction. The accumulated happiness that would have been achieved on average over the remaining expected life years can be calculated for each person killed in a war. This procedure assumes that the determinants of individual happiness are known and understood. Moreover, it assumes that the relationship between the determining factors and happiness in the future remains the same as it was in the estimation period of the past.

This approach is possible, but it is difficult to implement. First, the future happiness of a person is estimated, based on characteristics such as age, socio-economic background, education, health, expected income, and length of life. Second, these characteristics have to be associated with the persons who died in war. This procedure can result in major errors. In particular, if the dead have characteristics not included in the estimation of happiness in the first step, the estimates may be seriously biased. For example, it may well be that young soldiers killed on the battlefield are more optimistic and idealistic than average. As these characteristics are positively related to happiness, a standard empirical approach would systematically underestimate the future happiness lost. Military conflict would then appear to be less damaging to happiness than it is in reality. In contrast, if mainly pessimistic and materialistic persons die during wars, the future well-being lost by the dead is overestimated by the econometric estimate of happiness.

It should be noted that an aggregate happiness indicator that includes the well-being lost by those killed is no longer related to the population living. The more people that die during a war, the more strongly a country's happiness indicator is purely the effect of calculation rather than of direct observation via representative surveys. Moreover, estimates of happiness tend to lack credibility when the data basis, the living population, is small relative to the number of people killed in military conflict. The estimates of happiness may deviate strongly from what is relevant for the dead, so the calculation of the well-being lost by the dead is unreliable.

Calculating happiness on the basis of econometric estimates faces an additional problem. Such calculations offer a particularly wide scope for governments to influence the happiness indicator in their favour. A malevolent government may even engage in a military conflict with the aim of getting rid of the unhappy part of their population. The happiness indicator would thus rise, and based on the happiness indicator, the government could claim that it had improved the well-being of its population.

Disregarding the Well-Being of the Dead by Definition

Instead of trying to calculate the well-being lost by the victims of war, their well-being can be excluded from the happiness count by assuming that a country's happiness indicator refers only to the living. If the dead had the same happiness level on average as the rest of the population, it would not matter for average well-being if the dead are disregarded. But this assumption is dubious; the dead may well have been individuals with a particularly high or low future happiness potential. In that case, the negative effect on happiness of military conflict is under- or overestimated, respectively.

Taking into account the grief, suffering, and mourning of parents, children, other relatives, and friends of the deceased can capture one part of the unhappiness created by war. Empirical research suggests that the psychological costs of losing a relative or friend are substantial. The largest emotional loss occurs from the death of a spouse; the second-worst loss comes from the death of a child; and the third-worst arises from the death of a parent. The grief continues for many years. It may well be that grief about a departed person is immense to others but that the individual in question wanted to die because he or she did not expect any happiness in the future.

These empirical results refer to the loss of people under peaceful conditions in present-day developed economies. It can only be speculated how much a person killed is mourned in times of war. A soldier killed may have yearned for a long and happy life but his relatives and friends do not mourn his death because they believe that the death was in favour of a "good" or even "holy" cause. Others may even rejoice and increase their level of happiness about what they consider to be a "martyr". In this case, war raises happiness rather than reducing it.

A major result of empirical happiness research is that people adjust to good and bad experiences. There is a tendency to return to a "set point" of happiness determined by genetic factors. The speed and extent of adjustment varies between areas and individuals. The question is whether people are able to adjust to war experiences. The finding that the change in the number of victims, rather than their absolute number, reduces well-being in civil wars suggests that people adjust to the horrors of war to some extent. The experience that many people die in wars may make the fact that one's son, husband, father, other relative, or acquaintance has died more bearable. But should this adaptation to such terrible conditions be considered a reduction of unhappiness? Should we take war to be less brutal and devastating just because people get used to it? It seems that few people would wish to accept a military conflict knowing that they would become accustomed to the immense sufferings it would entail. However, to ignore the process of adaptation is not a convincing solution either, because it conflicts with empirical observations.

The Case of Terrorism

Terrorism is a special type of war in which the civil population is targeted and the goal is to create havoc and produce fear. Estimating the happiness of countries affected by terrorism reveals that more intense terrorist activity in terms of the number of attacks and of victims more severely reduces the life satisfaction of the population. For Northern Ireland, the well-being cost from one additional terror victim is equivalent to about 0.6 per cent of income.

The attacks of 9/11 revealed to have produced large psychological cost, which may substantially exceed the physical harm. The reason is that fear constitutes a significant part of the risks of terrorism. Surveys of random samples of the general population have found that people would be willing to pay nearly twice as much for a reduction in deaths from terrorism as they would for an equivalent reduction in deaths from natural disasters. The effect of a terrorist attack also reduces individual well-being beyond the country attacked. The mental distress produced in the population of the United Kingdom is roughly thirty per cent of the negative impact of widowhood, and almost twenty per cent of becoming unemployed.

A study of civil wars was conducted comprising 44 countries around the year 2000 and based on average happiness by country from representative surveys. Its findings suggest that military conflicts significantly and strongly reduce the well-being of the population. The direct effects of suffering, fear, and agony are larger than the indirect effects due to reductions in income caused by civil wars. The evidence on aggregate happiness in the various countries presented in Chap. 2 supports this finding. Nations such as Ukraine, Afghanistan, Yemen, and South Sudan, which are all involved in civil unrest and international wars, are among the countries with the lowest happiness levels in the world.

Military Conflict May Raise Happiness

Some people experience war as energizing and even addictive. The concept of "ennobling" war has been cherished in many cultures, for instance among classical Greek soldiers, medieval knights in Europe, and samurais in Japan. Many military conflicts have been termed "good" wars because they were proclaimed to serve a desirable goal. This holds not only for "holy" wars by Christian crusaders and the Jihad by Muslims but also for revolutionary wars in America and Europe, the two World Wars, and the wars in Vietnam, Iraq, and Afghanistan. People fighting in these wars, and civilians affected by it, may convert the costs of war into psychological benefits—a rather surprising turn-around.

Persons who have experienced war often refer to a feeling of happiness that arises from the solidarity war engenders, and even more importantly from a sense of common effort and shared purpose. War provides a purpose in life that is otherwise missing for a significant number of people. As a result, war is experienced by these people as a relief. During wars the number of suicides diminishes because the military conflict overrides personal problems.

Another reason why war experiences can in retrospect appear to be positive may be what could be called “afterglow”. After terrible events, people are glad to have survived. They then begin to reconstruct their past in a positive light and look at it as a great experience. This is a very special form of remembering.

It may be hypothesized that the type of military conflict and the expectations about its outcome may also influence how happiness is affected. When young men are drafted compulsorily, the conflict may be experienced as positive as long as people expect to be on the winning side. But as soon as this expectation turns negative, the casualties and other burdens of war are likely to be felt in a much more negative way. These effects are mitigated in the case of professional soldiers, provided they bear the brunt of the conflict. They are mitigated even more if foreign mercenaries are used.

War also raises happiness by producing short-run “combat flow”. Such an effect is sometimes reported for combat situations, in which it contributes to both the well-being and the effectiveness of soldiers. Addiction to the experience of combat flow has been documented for the Vietnam War, but there is also evidence going back to Homeric Greece and Medieval Europe. Noted authors, such as Tolstoy in *War and Peace* (1865–68) for the Napoleonic period and Jünger in his book *In Stahlgewittern* (1920) for World War I, extensively report instances of combat flow. In the dreadful battles of the First World War, “trench humour” was sometimes observed, and some authors go so far as to speak of a “lovely war”. Soldiers experienced satisfaction in killing, supporting the notion of “combat flow”.

These forms of happiness in war could be dismissed as inappropriate for moral reasons and disregarded completely. Scholars such as John Harsanyi, Amartya Sen, and earlier John Stuart Mill argue that “sadistic and malicious” pleasures need to be excluded from the social welfare function. It would indeed be dangerous to justify any war by the fact that it was waged by an army of happy soldiers high on combat flow. Such a view is in line with much of classical Greek philosophy; for instance, Epicurus argued that there may be combat flow but that it always has to be subordinate to the greater goal of achieving peace. Similar ideas can be attributed to Socrates, Plato and Aristotle with their notion of eudaimonia (see Chap. 2).

However, totally neglecting these forms of happiness because they are unethical is somewhat drastic. To do so is to disregard empirically well-documented feelings of happiness in and after conflict. Positively valued experiences such as shared purpose, solidarity, trust, friendship, and national pride should not be ignored. But it is important to differentiate immediate pleasures such as combat flow from the summum bonum, or supreme good, of real happiness. Subjective feelings are not always a good indicator of what can be taken to be “true” happiness.

Psychological Costs of Military Combat

While combat flow raises the well-being of the soldiers experiencing it in the short run, there is strong evidence that military service in combat strongly reduces the long-run well-being even of the soldiers who survive. Many soldiers are affected by post-traumatic stress disorder, which manifests itself in higher rates of crime, violence, and suicide and in a greater take-up of disability benefits among veterans. Survey evidence of soldiers who served in combat zones finds that one quarter of active soldiers returning from service in Iraq and Afghanistan experience lower well-being and suffer from depression, drug and alcohol dependency, homelessness, and suicidal thoughts.

So far, most of these studies have been descriptive. Most of them compare experiences in war to a civilian comparison group, which may have quite different underlying levels of subjective individual well-being. It may be that individuals who engage in war are less happy than those who stay out of it. There is thus a causality problem: Does war make participants unhappy, or do unhappy people engage in war? This question can be approached by considering the draft lotteries used in the United States for World War II, the Korean War, and the Vietnam War. The individuals drafted are a random choice, so both happy and unhappy people were drafted. Interestingly, the studies overcoming the causality problem come to the same result as the descriptive studies: draft exposure tends to affect health adversely, and there is an increased risk of suicide, automobile accidents, and mortality due to military-induced smoking. A refined study for the United States and the wars in Iraq and Afghanistan controlled for the mental health of soldiers prior to deployment and exploited also the variation in exposure to combat. It finds that combat service raises the risk of suicide and post-traumatic stress disorder. Mental health problems occur in particular if a person was exposed to frequent enemy fire, was injured, or observed the death or wounding of a comrade or non-combatant.

Concluding Remarks

It may be argued that the conception of life satisfaction or happiness used in econometric studies, as a simple sensation composed of variations along a unique quantitative dimension, is faulty. Psychologists and economists have borrowed the concept from Jeremy Bentham, but such philosophers as Plato, Aristotle, and James Stuart Mill employ a much richer idea called eudaimonia. It refers to a broad and multidimensional concept of human flourishing rather than a simple "hedonic flow". While this criticism must be taken seriously, the advantages of a unidimensional scale of subjective individual well-being should not be overlooked. Such a scale correlates highly with objective indicators such as positively with laughing, optimism, and social integration, and negatively with suicide. These uni-dimensional estimates of happiness provide us with useful insights about the determinants of happiness. This can also be expected to be the case if military conflicts are more extensively studied among the determinants of subjective well-being.

The discussion reveals that analysing the effect of war on happiness elicits deep issues going far beyond one particular academic discipline, in particular far beyond economics. Only serious interdisciplinary exchange and discussion can help us resolve these issues. The basic questions, of course, have a long history. They appear in a particularly striking way when studying how war affects happiness. What is new is the emphasis on empirical evidence—an aspect generally absent in philosophical discourse on the theme. Looking at the effects of military conflict on individual well-being by econometrically analysing data may help us to reconsider some aspects and to see them in a new light. It may also contribute to better understanding what "subjective well-being" or "happiness" means under the particular conditions of wartime.

Literature

The discussion is based on:
Frey, Bruno S. 2012. Well-Being and War. *International Review of Economics* 59 (4): 363–375.

A general empirical analysis of adaptation is provided in:
Clark, Andrew E., Ed Diener, Yannis Georgellis, and Richard E. Lucas. 2008. Lags and Leads in Life Satisfaction: A Test of the Baseline Hypothesis. *Economic Journal* 118 (529): F222–F243.

The psychological cost of losing relatives or friends are calculated by:
Oswald, Andrew J., and Nattavudh Powdthavee. 2008. Death, Happiness, and the Calculation of Compensatory Damages. *Journal of Legal Studies* 37 (S2): S217–S251.

A general study of the welfare effects on the victims of war is provided in:
Welsch, Heinz. 2008. The Social Cost of Civil Conflict: Evidence from Surveys of Happiness. *Kyklos* 61 (2): 320–340.

The case of terrorism is studied in:
Frey, Bruno S., Simon Luechinger, and Alois Stutzer. 2007. Calculating Tragedy: Assessing the Costs of Terrorism. *Journal of Economic Surveys* 21 (1): 1–24.

The concept of combat flow is treated in:
Harari, Yuval N. 2008. Combat Flow: Military, Political, and Ethical Dimensions of Subjective Well-Being in War. *Review of General Psychology* 12 (3): 253–264.

Fundamental issues of how to deal with moral aspects of human welfare are discussed in:
Sen, Amartya. 2009. *The Idea of Justice*. London: Penguin.

Chapter 14
Happiness in the Digital World

Abstract Spending a large number of hours on the Internet has positive and negative effects on subjective well-being. Social network users tend to compare their income to those with whom they interact, leading to less satisfaction with their own income. People with a strong inclination to be "liked" on Facebook are less satisfied with the life they lead and feel lonelier. Hours spent on online social networks are negatively correlated with happiness. The overall consequences on subjective well-being of these far-reaching digital developments are yet unknown.

Internet Use

Many people all over the world have access to the Internet and spend a large number of hours with it. Its effects on subjective well-being are divergent. Some studies find positive effects on individuals' social interactions; they visit theatres, opera, and art exhibitions and meet relatives, friends, and acquaintances more often. Based on an aggregate index of digitization taking into account aspects such as ubiquity, price, reliability and speed it has been claimed that a higher level of this index is associated with higher life satisfaction. But this only holds once a certain level of digitization has been reached.

On the other hand, trust in other people seems to be reduced, which hampers happiness. One reason is that the Internet reduces self-regulation and self-awareness, which increases aggressive and offensive behaviours in face-to-face interactions. People who regularly visit the Internet as a source of information derive lower satisfaction from their income. This effect can be attributed to reducing people's life satisfaction when they compare their own income with that of other people.

The use of social network sites has strongly increased over the last decade. Facebook is by far the most popular online social network and is used by no less than seventy-one per cent of US Americans. Multi-platform use is as well increasing markedly. Social network users are more likely to compare their income to those with whom they interact, leading to less satisfaction with their own income. In addition, self-esteem is hampered. People with a strong inclination to be "liked" on Facebook

B. S. Frey, *Economics of Happiness*, SpringerBriefs in Economics,
https://doi.org/10.1007/978-3-319-75807-7_14

are less satisfied with the life they lead. Empirical evidence points to a negative association between the hours spent on an online social network and happiness; users indeed feel lonelier.

The digital world has also led to mass surveillance of everyone, not only actual or suspected terrorists. The secret services of many countries, in particular the American CIA, FBI, NSA and others, have spent billions of dollars to infiltrate our computers, smart phones, TVs and cars on a regular basis. The large digital firms located in the Silicon Valley—Google, Facebook, Twitter, Amazon, Microsoft and Apple—each day syphon off terabytes of data from ordinary consumers and users of the Internet. Indeed, most people have a "digital double", a black box fed with our personal data but without our permission.

Social bots, or robotic bloggers, influence and distort our views about consumer goods and services and politics in a much stronger way than propaganda and censorship did in the past. Digital technology threatens democracy, which many techies consider to be outmoded, and tends to replace it by a data-driven benevolent dictatorship. The most extreme development has occurred in the People's Republic of China. The "citizen score" reduces all the data collected about a person to a single number summarizing your activities as employee, in your leisure time, on social networks, and above all as a citizen. For instance, a person who reads negative reports about the Chinese government or who has friends of friends that criticize the government will lose points on his or her citizen score. This negatively affects the jobs offered, raises the interest rate for loans, and makes it more difficult to travel outside China. This neo-feudal society has not yet fully reached democratic societies. However, the "credit scores" collected in the United States and elsewhere are to some extent similar, as they determine not only opportunities in the financial sector but go far beyond. The consequences for subjective well-being of these far-reaching digital developments are yet unknown. Many people are only partly or not at all aware of the restriction of their personal freedom and thus of their happiness. This influence may so far have been neglected and therefore be underestimated.

Literature

Helbing, Dirk. 2015. *Thinking Ahead. Essays on Big Data, Digital Revolution, and Participatory Market Society.* Cham: Springer.

Pasquale, Frank. 2016. *The Black Box Society: The Secret Algorithms That Control Money and Information.* Cambridge, MA: Harvard University Press.

A positive relationship between an aggregate index of digitization and life satisfaction has been suggested by:

Katz, Raul L., and Pantelis Koutroumpis. 2013. Measuring Digitization: A Growth and Welfare Multiplier. *Technovation* 33 (10): 314–319.

Negative effects have been found by:

Sabatini, Fabio, and Francesco Sarracino. 2017. Online Networks and Subjective Well-Being. *Kyklos* 70 (3): 456–480.

Chapter 15
Beyond Material Aspects

Abstract These are the most important insights of modern happiness research: People with higher income are happier, but this effect becomes weaker and weaker as income rises. Good social relationships, physical and psychological health, and democracy as well as decentralized political decision-making raise happiness. Several insights of happiness research are inconsistent with human beings being rational and egotistic: Unemployed people are much less satisfied with their lives even though they have more leisure time. Self-employed people work harder, but thanks to higher autonomy report being happier. People who care for others by donating money and engaging in voluntary work are happier. Human well-being is no longer intimately connected with the provision of material goods. Material aspects are not to be neglected, but self-determined work is of crucial importance for happiness.

Expected and Unexpected Insights

Happiness research in recent years has accumulated fascinating and important results. Among the most important are:

- People with higher income consider themselves to be happier than people with lower income; they enjoy a higher level of life satisfaction. But higher income raises happiness less and less. Human beings quite rapidly adjust to higher income. In addition, they compare themselves mostly with higher income people, a tendency that reduces the happiness level.
- One of the most important factors conducive to happiness is good social relationships. People who have close friends and engage in intensive family relationships are more satisfied with their lives than are more isolated people.
- Good physical and psychological health are major contributors to happiness. The reverse also holds: Happy people are less affected by contagious diseases.
- People who enjoy the privilege of living in a democracy and with decentralized political decision-making report that they are happier.

Some of these results from well-being research do not necessarily correspond to common sense. Thus, it is often taken as obvious that people in less developed countries

B. S. Frey, *Economics of Happiness*, SpringerBriefs in Economics,
https://doi.org/10.1007/978-3-319-75807-7_15

are happier than those in nations with a higher per-capita income. However, empirical research using many different happiness data convincingly demonstrates that living in an economically more advanced country contributes strongly to subjective well-being. With higher income, one is to some extent protected against the troubles of ordinary life. People are not constantly forced to think about how to survive, or even to find sufficient money to buy food, let alone larger expenditures such as for household appliances.

Some important insights of happiness research are inconsistent with the idea of human beings who are solely governed by rationality and egoism. Three results illustrate this conclusion.

- Unemployed people are much less satisfied with their lives than those working. This finding applies even if the unemployed to not suffer a reduction in their income. In principle, the unemployed should therefore be happier as they do not have to work but have more leisure time.
- Self-employed people work more hours and do so more intensively than people employed in firms and other organizations. Moreover they have lower average income and have to cope with higher risk. Nevertheless, the self-employed report that they are happier because they enjoy more autonomy.
- People who donate money and engage in voluntary work are happier than those who care less for other people or have fewer opportunities to do so.

For a long time, human welfare was dominated by economic activities. Past generations were in this respect much worse off than the present generation. Gross national income as the measure of the extent of economic activities was more closely related to life satisfaction up to recent times than it is today. This close correlation is still true for poor countries.

Recently human well-being is no longer so intimately connected with the provision of material goods. Other aspects of life have become more important. Modern happiness research in economics and psychology empirically shows that while material aspects are not to be neglected, self-determined work characterized by autonomy and participation rights and intensive social contacts are of crucial importance for happiness.

A reasonable economic and social policy must take these fundamental changes into account. But government policy should not try to directly determine people's happiness. This should be done in an indirect way so that individuals can achieve happiness in their own ways. The constitutional level, where the fundamental rules of human interaction are determined, should open the road to more democratic participation rights, in particular through popular initiatives and referendums. Political decisions should be taken at a decentralized level, as close as possible to the citizens affected. In current politico-economic decisions, human beings should be given a greater scope to attain their own idea of happiness.

Literature

Frey, Bruno S., Jana Gallus, and Lasse Steiner. 2014. Open Issues in Happiness Research. *International Review of Economics* 61 (2): 115–125.
Kay, John. 2012. *Obliquity. Why Our Goals Are Best Achieved Indirectly*. London: Penguin.